Common Sense
LEADERSHIP

Garth Johns

BALBOA.
PRESS
A DIVISION OF HAY HOUSE

Balboa Press books may be ordered through booksellers or by contacting:

Balboa Press
A Division of Hay House
1663 Liberty Drive
Bloomington, IN 47403
www.balboapress.com
1-(877) 407-4847

ISBN: 978-1-4525-7348-9 (sc)
ISBN: 978-1-4525-7350-2 (hc)
ISBN: 978-1-4525-7349-6 (e)

Library of Congress Control Number: 2013907688

Printed in the United States of America.

Balboa Press rev. date: 05/13/2013

Acknowledgements

At some point in the last year or two, I felt that Common Sense Leadership, originally published in 2009, needed to be updated. There was nothing fundamentally wrong with it but having presented the principles on many occasions and having enjoyed the opportunity to observe my principles in action, I felt compelled to change some of the material and add a chapter or two, all of which was intended to improve the overall quality of the book. Although it may be claimed that I am a bit biased in this regard, I sincerely believe we have been successful.

My thanks remain with all those who contributed to the first edition. In addition, I want to thanks Beth McAuley for her fine editing job, Dan Carter and Doug Schneider as wonderful colleagues who were there for me when I needed to kick some new ideas around. Dave Dawson has been pushing me, not only on this edition but also, on the upcoming Equine Edition. My thanks go out to Heather, Andrea, Wendy, Kimberley and their respective teams at Balboa Press for their assistance and support. The final product is a testament to their outstanding work. These are exciting times for me and I thank all of these fine folks plus likely scores of others whom I have unintentionally forgotten.

Finally, I want to thank my family for all their understanding and support. My daughters Julie, Andrea and Heather together with son-in-laws Doug and Phil and our grandchildren Chad, Meredith and now Keaton. Hopefully, I inspire you with common sense leadership because I know you all make my life so much more meaningful. And as I said in the first edition, none of this would be possible without my confidante, my inspiration, my love and my best friend, my wife of 38 years (and counting), Debi.

Contents

Introduction

Leadership is not a role reserved for presidents, prime ministers or CEO's. All of us have the opportunity to be leaders, inspiring others to improve themselves in so many ways. This does not simply apply to the workplace but it applies at home, in the community and at work.

In 2009, I enjoyed the thrill of publishing my first book *Common Sense Leadership.* Looking back on that time, I now realize that I had so much to learn. I started out believing that I would be addressing one narrow group of readers, and I changed part way along the journey to broaden the scope of my intended audience. Ultimately, I realized that the principles I was espousing applied to everyone. In fact, I discovered that each one of us, in our own way, is a leader. The only question to be answered now is "what is the extent of leadership provided by each of us?"

For years, I had read, learned, written and presented on the topic of leadership and somehow believed that I knew everything there was to know about the topic. However, the light truly came on one day when I came home from work to see the excitement in my grandson's eyes and hear it in his voice when he announced that he had learned to print his name. Trying to sound equally excited, I said, "WOW!! Where did you learn that?" The answer he gave is, in itself, immaterial. Whether he had learned this skill from his parents or his day-care provider or his grandmother mattered less than the fact that someone had inspired him to grow beyond where he had been. It was that realization that led me to establish my very simple definition of leadership—**a leader is one who inspires others to achieve greater personal heights or higher levels of performance.**

In fact, I have come to believe so strongly in this definition that I have started to see, on a daily basis, evidence to support my contention that we are all leaders. The role of leadership can never be left exclusively to noteworthy individuals such as Nelson Mandela, Mother Teresa, Barack Obama, Bill Gates or other such high-profile personalities. Leadership is not a birthright nor is it defined by our titles at work or in the community. It is determined solely by our everyday actions. In that regard, managers, union leaders, parents, hockey coaches, choir masters, service club presidents, school teachers and so many others are all leaders because they serve to inspire somebody else. Now, let's be clear, I am well aware of the millions who currently reside in prisons, all of the delinquent or deadbeat parents plus an assortment of other ne'er-do-wells or malcontents who seemingly contribute so little to the betterment of the world. However, they are clearly in the minority. For the rest of us, we can each play a role as leader to somebody else, be it in our workplace, with our family, in our community, as part of our union and so on. We all have the opportunity to inspire someone else. Leadership is really a matter of degree and so, we can choose to inspire others just a bit or extensively. How much is up to each of us in turn.

It is with this in mind that I decided to revisit the principles in *Common Sense Leadership*. They are as true and important today as they were when I first published them. In fact, I believe in them more firmly than ever, and so I have added one new principle that relates to the nature of "professionalism" and what it means to all of us. These principles, if followed, can help us become better managers, parents, volunteers, community members and leaders. Unfortunately, there are no guarantees and, like life, leadership is one continuous journey. As I have discovered, writing and speaking about these principles has not made me impervious to the slips and falls along the way. Occasionally, I need to remind myself to practise what I am preaching.

Finally, it is my view that our lives can generally be divided into three stages. The first stage occurs when we are growing and developing physically, mentally, emotionally and spiritually as young men and women. The second stage includes the time that we spend establishing ourselves in our career, our community and our lives. Some of us get married and perhaps have children. For most of us, we build homes and we spend significant time determining what it is that defines who we are. The third stage is for reflection and giving back to our families, our professions and our communities. We become teachers, coaches, mentors and are better prepared to share with others the wisdom that our years have granted us. It is this final stage that I personally have grown into. This book reflects the learnings I have gained over the years through formal channels at many post-secondary institutions in Canada and the U.S. More importantly, it reflects many of the lessons I have been taught by life, my work experiences and exposure to so many good, kind and wise people. This is my opportunity to share these learnings with those of you who are ready to receive them.

While the 11 principles I discuss in my book apply to all aspects of life at home, at work and in the community, I have dedicated the first chapter to the workplace, turning some attention to the differences between management and leadership. Unfortunately, there are still far too many individuals who see these two roles as being one and the same. In addition, I have added a new chapter which is dedicated to a discussion about what it means to be a professional. While, at first blush, one may be inclined to see this as another chapter on workplace issues, being a professional means conducting yourself in a way that demonstrates certain characteristics and values. These characteristics and values will always be meaningful at work but they have just as much significance at home and in the community. Can stay-at-home parents behave in a professional fashion? Of course they can.

More than ever, I believe in these 11 principles, and in this revised edition I have added more substance to each one of them and provided better examples. In the final analysis, there are those who wish to know how they can inspire their families, their colleagues and their community. They don't worry about achieving fame, fortune and greatness, for those who achieve such fame and fortune may be limited to a relative handful of individuals; instead, they focus on simply inspiring others.

So often, we seem to feel if we are going through the routine of our life as if we act in isolation of everybody else. And yet, in so many ways and in so many instances, somebody is always observing us. It may be our colleagues at work, our staff, our children, our friends or our neighbours. If we always conduct ourselves, believing that somebody is watching and assessing us, there will be a greater likelihood that our actions may just serve to inspire them. Children watch when we use our manners or when we are kind to other people or animals. Our staff and colleagues see when we treat others with respect and courtesy or when we leave bad attitudes and anger at the door. The waitress who serves us coffee notes when we smile or when we show appreciation for good service. Alternatively, there is always someone watching or affected by us when we throw a cigarette butt out the car window or toss our garbage onto the street, when we are nasty or disrespectful to others. There is always a price to be paid for illegal or unethical conduct. Our attitude and our actions are what will ultimately make us true leaders that inspire others and provide a role model to follow.

For all of us, my sincerest belief is that to be better, more inspirational leaders, all we need to worry about is following and sharing my 11 principles for effective leadership discussed in this book and encourage others we meet to follow them too. How we influence others is often not seen as an outstanding event or moment in time. In so many instances, it is our simplest gesture or action that can have the greatest effect on the lives of those around us. Here, then, are my 11 key principles:

1. Act like a professional at all times.
2. Enjoy what you do with your life.
3. Be nice to everyone you meet. It's really not that difficult.
4. Always act with integrity. It will help you sleep at night.
5. Always respect time.
6. Communicate regularly and effectively with everyone you meet.
7. Know your customers, whoever they may be.
8. Support one another. Be a team player.
9. Scan the horizon and be prepared for whatever may come your way.
10. You can't please all of the people all of the time so stop trying to. Make decisions.
11. Act with energy and enthusiasm. It tends to be infectious.

While many of the discussions contained herein relate to the workplace, the principles apply equally to all facets of our lives, not only at work but also at home and in the community. Just open your mind and heart to all the possibilities.

A Manager or a Leader?

Management 101

There are still too many people who just don't get it. The roles of management and leadership are not the same thing. Management, broadly speaking, is the performance of a bundle of duties, through the use of financial, capital and human resources in order to achieve or satisfy some or all of the operational needs of a company or organization. While the specifics may vary from one management position to another, generally, it involves activities such as planning, organizing, implementing, delegating, controlling and measuring.

An example of a typical managerial job description may include (at least in part) the following key responsibilities and duties. Remember, this is from an actual job description and, while it has been reduced to its key components, it is not made up.

1. Manage, co-ordinate and administrate the implementation of new initiatives, special projects and programs by:
   * Managing, assigning and coordinating . . .
   * Preparing and reviewing specifications . . . .
   * Planning, coordinating and updating . . .
   * Providing technical advice, supervision and management over all projects . . .
   * Providing reports and presentations to . . .
   * Managing future operations
   * Reviewing and approving consultant agreements . . .

2. Manage, coordinate and administrate . . . by:
   - Directing, controlling and overseeing . . .
   - Supervising development of adequate promotional and educational programs . . .
   - Supervising formal audits and studies . . .
   - Managing . . .
   - Reviewing and approving . . .
3. Provide professional advisory services by:
   - Organizing, assigning and providing direction to staff . . .
   - Investigating and taking appropriate action in response to complaints . . .
   - Recommending actions . . .
   - Consulting with and providing advice to . . .
   - Reviewing staff reports . . .
4. Manage annual budget . . .
5. Manage and oversee development . . .
6. Develop policies . . .
7. Work in accordance with provisions of applicable health and safety . . .

I have cut the full job description short because the point has been made. The key duties are seen to be essentially managerial in nature. It is, after all, a management position.

In my early teachings, I had promoted a traditional model of management which was defined by the following activities:

1. Forecasting and planning. Managers must plan for the future using the best information they have at their disposal. These activities include strategic planning, budgeting, determining future departmental goals and the resource needs to achieve those goals.
2. Building organizations and systems. The workplace needs to be organized so it operates as efficiently as possible. This includes activities such as recruiting properly trained staff and engaging systems that allow the organization to deal with any and all needs and contingencies.

3. Directing subordinates. Managers need to communicate with staff, supervise them and ensure that their actions and behaviour are consistent with company policies.
4. Coordinating various activities across the business such that the work of each organizational entity should complement and enrich the work of all the others.
5. Guiding and controlling those activities so that all parts of the business are working towards the same end. As such, managers observe, measure and report on any deviations with a view to taking steps to correct such deviations and getting the unit back on track.

However, I came to appreciate that none of this included the importance of what we now call "the soft skills" so badly needed to manage effectively. These skills have become increasingly important as we attempt to move managers from a point of being simple technicians to professionals who require a vast array of skills and talents to be effective in their jobs. And yet, even today, so many fail to understand how significant these soft skills are to the art of management. While managers still need to plan, organize, implement, delegate, control and measure, the best way they can do it is by building relationships, motivating, coaching, mentoring and developing staff. That is what has become increasingly critical. As such, we are expecting them to no longer be just managers but now, leaders as well.

Going back to the job description mentioned above, it reflects many of the activities that we generally consider to be part of the role as performed by managers. Therefore, they

- manage, assign, coordinate resources
- prepare, review, plan
- provide technical advice, reports and presentations
- review and approve agreements
- direct, control, oversee, supervise, approve, determine, organize, assign
- investigate, recommend, consult, control expenditures, analyse, monitor

In fact, when we examine the qualifications outlined in the job description, our attention is turned to "hard skills" of degrees, a background in that particular field and administration, communications skills, demonstrated concern for safety, customer service, team assignments, supervision, labour relations and financial responsibility. Eventually, mention is made of the competencies of "coaching, leading, mediating, negotiating and facilitation, team building and mentoring skills." However, these "soft skills" are deeply hidden in the description of requirements.

A quick search of posted vacancies on any major job search website will reveal the same type of pattern. Selection criteria, in the majority of cases, focus on technical skills, with relatively little in the way of interpersonal and leadership skills being mentioned. It could lead one to postulate that technical skills are more easily determined, measured and identified or perhaps considered to be even more important than interpersonal or leadership skills. In other words, it is easier to review applications and interview for skills such as experience with computer applications, knowledge of contract administration, project management skills, payroll experience, engineering degrees, and CA designation than it is to evaluate intangibles such as the ability to lead, motivate and inspire.

So, what is wrong with this picture? Is this not the essence of management? If it walks like a duck and talks like a duck, what else can it be? A manager is expected to manage, which includes organizing, planning, implementing, delegating, controlling and measuring. Should we be concerned about leadership? Perhaps managers can be something more than just managers. Perhaps, they can be leaders for their staff. To answer these questions, we must have a closer look at what leadership at work really means.

Leadership 101

So often, it seems that leadership is solely within the purview and playground of the CAOs, CEOs, presidents, vice-presidents and other such significant players in our organizations. Can the front-line manager really be a leader? Can the recreation director be more than just a manager who plans, organizes, implements, delegates and controls? What about the nurse manager? The fire chief? The director of HR? What about anybody who is expected to manage and, more importantly, to lead others whether they be staff, volunteers, students or members of our own family?

I firmly believe that there is the very real possibility that front-line managers can be and should be something more than just managers. Of course they can be leaders, but the problem is that we expect them to serve first and foremost in the role that defines what they do. A number of years ago, after interviewing a number of the best managers who were considered to be the "cream of the crop" by their respective employers, I explored their role as leaders rather than managers, and the results were rather eye-opening. These people were considered to be the front-line stars of their organizations, many with prospects of becoming the future senior leaders. Curiously enough, discussions about their roles as managers received only cursory consideration. Instead, they saw themselves as current leaders of their people with a strong focus on "leading" responsibilities. While they all placed differing emphasis on different functions, it was fascinating to note the commonality of the words they chose to describe their roles and the roles of their colleagues. In no particular order, they mentioned the importance of

- being approachable
- being a mentor
- having vision
- being a good communicator
- being a strong helmsman
- having passion for the job
- being the captain of the team
- being decisive
- being consistent
- promoting learning
- celebrating success
- having integrity
- remaining calm at all times
- demonstrating good common sense

- remaining humble
- being open to new initiatives
- empowering staff and leading by example

Indeed, these are characteristics of good leaders. There was very little discussion about their skills in budgeting or recruiting or their knowledge of scheduling of staff, transit systems or surgical procedures. They were clearly more excited and focused on their role as leaders. But was their enthusiasm for leadership being appreciated or was it possible that their organizational structures continued to push these managers into being simply managers?

What do we need to do to have all managers and not just the "cream of the crop" move to the next level and become true leaders? The answer? It needs to start with an organizational culture that encourages all staff to be leaders and to inspire one another. For the purposes of this discussion, we need managers to be leaders and to inspire their staff, their colleagues on the management teams and the organization as a whole. So how do we begin to change the organizational culture? Regardless of how big or small you are, it begins with your organization's mission, vision and values, and these must be more than nice words. They have to be translated into action.

Mission Statements

Most contemporary organizations have established mission statements that describe the fundamental purpose of their existence. The statement is usually quite short and states why they are here, what they do, who they serve and why they bother in the first place. An example of a good mission statement comes from the Canadian Cancer Society, which says simply:

The Canadian Cancer Society is a national, community-based organization of volunteers whose mission is the eradication of cancer and the enhancement of the quality of life of people living with cancer.

If all staff and managers are well aware of this mission, they can tailor all of their activities and decisions to ensure that the mission is satisfied. It serves as an excellent guidepost. Please note that this mission statement says nothing about what different divisions or departments use as their overarching mission. The entire organization is captured by one simple statement. If the entire leadership team follows it, it may eliminate the growth of silos and other competitive interests within the organization.

Vision Statements

The organizational vision, like the mission statement, is usually short and sweet and describes what the organization hopes to look like at some point in the future, that point being 5 or 10 years away. Notwithstanding the futuristic view taken, it should maintain the essence of the described mission and bring all parts of the organization together to rally for one common strategic direction. This "vision" allows all employees to see how their efforts contribute to some greater, anticipated good for the organization. They are no longer putting nuts on bolts but rather building cars that will be the best cars built on the planet (or some such thing). The vision statement needs to be inspiring for all members of the organization.

Let's consider the vision statements of some of the better known and more successful organizations:

- To be number one or number two in every business we are engaged in. (General Electric)
- Continually finding new ways to generate superior earnings through Koch's core capabilities: MBM, operations excellence, trading, transaction excellence, public sector. (Koch Industries MBM)
- To be the most innovative enterprise and the preferred supplier. (3M)
- To be led by a globally diverse workforce that consistently delivers outstanding business results, understands the various cultural demands of a global marketplace, is passionate about technology and the promise it holds to tap human potential and thrives in a corporate culture where inclusive behaviors are valued. (Microsoft)

- Apple is committed to bringing the best personal computing experience to students, educators, creative professionals and consumers around the world through its innovative hardware, software and Internet offerings. (Apple)

While a casual observer may not be inspired by any one of these statements, they must be meaningful to the employees of the respective firms. That is what is really important. Peter Senge, the director of the Center for Organizational Learning at the MIT Sloan School of Management, points out that getting the words right leads to beautiful, even inspiring, vision statements, but it's not what the vision is, it's what the vision does that matters. If done properly, visions and other guiding ideas can be tools for mobilizing and focusing energy of your people. The quality of vision statements can only be judged by their impact, not by how they sound.[1]

Values

Every organization should have a set of core values. Stop and think about this and consider the words CORE VALUES. These are the ideologies that we expect every employee to follow religiously in any activity that they are engaged in on behalf of the employer. There should be four or five core values that are meaningful and memorable. Like vision statements, they cannot simply be words that are politically correct and that sound very nice. If they are just words on paper, they will soon be forgotten. I have seen too many organizations that seem to believe they need to state something that looks good for the annual report or good for public relations or good for their public image and they decide (without sufficient input from staff or other stakeholders) to use words that sound particularly appealing. When this happens, their values fail to inspire anybody.

However, good value statements may be inspiring. Consider 3M for example. The company's motto is "innovative and practical solutions . . . from a diversified technology company." The company's values are as follows:

- To provide investors an attractive return through sustained quality growth.
- To satisfy customers with superior quality, value and service.
- To respect our social and physical environment.
- To be a company employees are proud to be a part of.

Other examples of sound organizational core values (in part) include:

- **Fun**—We believe humor is essential to success. We applaud irreverence and don't take ourselves too seriously. We celebrate achievement. We yodel. (Yahoo)
- **Customer Obsession**—(Our) Leaders start with the customer and work backwards. They work vigorously to earn and keep customer trust. Although leaders pay attention to competitors, they obsess over customers. (Amazon)
- **Excellence**—As a company, and as individuals, we value integrity, honesty, openness, personal excellence, constructive self-criticism, continual self-improvement, and mutual respect. (Microsoft)
- **Transparency**—We respond to the changing needs of residents and other organizations by providing transparent government within the framework of financial sustainability. (Regional Municipality of Durham)

In each of these samples, the values are simple, easy to understand and easy for staff to remember.

It is just as important that all organizations review and revisit their missions, visions and values occasionally. We cannot become so entrenched in these that we consider them to be permanent fixtures in our organizational world. In the private sector, the economic, competitive and technological worlds we work in are forever changing and we must be prepared to adapt as necessary. In the public sector, mission statements usually note that we have to meet the needs of our community. Consider politicians as a case in point. Politicians have a shelf life of four years, and while some may cast their minds and energies further down the road, many see themselves as being there to respond to the needs of the public, but in the end it is the public that decides who will address those issues on their behalf every four years. Should politicians have a vision of their own? Should organizational leaders in the private sector have a vision of their own or at least share one with their staff? Such visions could generate excitement and help focus the staff within the organization. In both the private and the public sectors, organizations must still understand what they are all about, where they are headed and what they hold near and dear in terms of core values.

So, if we understand that our organization needs to have a mission, a vision and core values, what will the leaders look like and what will they do? In all likelihood, there are thousands of volumes written about leadership and their actions, activities and characteristics. And for every volume written, there is a different definition of exactly what leadership is. Almost invariably, the examples used in those volumes will reflect Fortune 500 CEOs and presidents or inspirational leaders such as Ghandi, Nelson Mandela, Mother Theresa or Martin Luther King, Jr. What makes these people such outstanding leaders? More importantly, how does one go from being just an everyday manager to being a leader for her/his department and people?

There is no right or wrong answer. It is not a black or white issue, but rather a shade of grey. It can be circumstantial and it may vary from one industry or one employer to the next. However, for our purposes, it appears that there are a number of common themes, as expressed by the experts and certainly supported by those I have interviewed over the years. So, what is it that differentiates a leader from a manager?

Jim Collins in "Good to Great" identifies five levels of leadership, in a hierarchical format, as follows:

1. **Highly Capable Individuals**—make productive contributions by virtue of their talent, knowledge, skills and work habits. They are the technicians, the ones who are adequate by virtue of their training, education and experience. They are not yet managers of any kind.

2. **Contributing Team Members**—not only are they technically strong but they are now strong team players.
3. **Competent Managers**—are effective at planning, organizing, implementing, delegating and achieving objectives.
4. **Effective Leaders**—have learned to build commitment and enjoy the support of their staff to achieve a clear and compelling vision.
5. **Level 5 Executive**—is able to build enduring greatness through a paradoxical blend of personal humility and personal will.[2]

It would seem obvious that not all organizational managers will become Level 5 Executives. However, our recruitment processes, if effective, should at the very least deliver competent managers to the organization (from outside or from within), and we can assume further that the staff we recruit will be very capable individuals. The emphasis must be on developing competent managers such that they become effective leaders, and we must ensure that the highly competent individuals we hire have the potential to become contributing team members. To that end, as part of any recruitment and development practices, one must expect all staff to demonstrate core competencies. Those core competencies will vary from one organization to the next. In one organization I worked with, all four core competencies were used for its staff, regardless of their level in the organization. These included the following:

- Be customer focused and strive for service excellence.
- Embrace innovation and learning.
- Engage in effective interpersonal communication.
- Demonstrate utmost professionalism at all times.

In addition to these core competencies, all managers are expected to practice four managerial competencies:

- Demonstrate leadership and change management.
- Excel at making effective decisions.
- Engage in the coaching, mentoring and developing of others.
- Be strategic thinkers.

Again, I stress that the words all sound good but they are only as meaningful as the results that the words generate on a day-to-day basis.

In addition to these examples of managerial competencies, there are eight characteristics that managers should be expected to demonstrate if they are to be seen as great leaders:

1. They must be visionary in a strategic and operational sense.
2. They are outstanding communicators.
3. They focus on perpetual learning for themselves and their staff.
4. They show evidence of consistent decision making using common sense.
5. They exude ethical conduct at all times.
6. They expect a customer focus in everything they do.
7. They build and maintain strong, empowered teams.
8. They provide organizational clarity in their divisions/departments that support organizational plans and values.

From my experience of over 38 years in consulting and senior leadership roles, I have identified a list of personal skills and attributes that are critical to an organizational leader's ongoing success. These include being down to earth, caring for others, being energetic and enthusiastic, showing respect, being trustworthy and, on occasion, demonstrating a touch of charisma. What I have since discovered is that when combined, all of these competencies and characteristics are captured in the essence of my 11 principles of common sense leadership. Curiously enough, and this is of critical importance, these principles apply not only to organizational leaders but leaders of all kinds, at work, at home and in the community.

Principle #1

Being a Professional

I was recently meeting my good friend Pastor Doug Schneider over lunch, seeking, as always, his very sage counsel on a number of matters. During our discussion, he asked me what it meant to be a professional. I responded that it did not come with certificates or titles, but rather could simply be seen as the behaviours or competencies that all professionals demonstrate in their day-to-day lives. At that point, the young lady who was serving us approached and we put the matter to the test. I asked her if she considered herself a professional. Without missing a beat, she said "yes." When I asked why or what made her a professional, she answered, "I do my job with excellence and I enjoy what I do." It was so simple, yet so profound. What made her a professional was the quality of her work combined with her attitude, approach and pure joy of what she did. It warmed my heart to hear of it.

If all leaders need to act as professionals and all of us are leaders, then what does it mean to be a professional? Unlike the waitress Doug and I spoke with, and without reflecting too long on the ramifications of this question, we might be inclined to describe a professional as someone who is good in their particular field of endeavour. In fact, they are usually so good that they get paid very well for what they do. For instance, a professional baseball player gets paid to play while an amateur does not. In most instances, the professional is at the highest possible level of performance in his sport. Similarly, a professional actor gets paid while the amateur does not and, for the most part, professional actors are considered to be the very best in the field. For others, the measure comes with education, experience and the passing of certain tests rather than delineation based upon professional versus amateur. There is no such thing as an amateur doctor, amateur lawyer, amateur architect or amateur engineer. Regardless of how we measure professionals, by skill, ability, education or certificates, there are certain standards that will help to identify the professional within all of us. No matter what our status, position, career choice or place in the community, there are behaviours we can engage in to demonstrate a degree of professionalism. Such behaviours apply whether you are a stay-at-home parent, a neurosurgeon or anything in between. The following is a list that provides a sense of professional behaviours and values that are considered by most observers to reflect a true professional. How do you measure up?

1. Be competent and always perform to the very best of your abilities. Dr. Martin Luther King Jr. once said, "If a man is called to be a street sweeper, he should sweep streets even as Michelangelo painted or Beethoven composed music, or Shakespeare wrote poetry. He should sweep streets so well that all the hosts of heaven and earth will pause to say, 'Here lived a great street sweeper who did his job well.' Competence is not always measured by degrees, certificates or membership in an organization. It also doesn't mean that you have to be No. 1 or No. 2 in the world in your field. We can't all be at the top. However, we can work hard to ensure that we are always competent in our role and are performing it to the very best of our capabilities. A stay-at-home mom can take pride in being competent at what she is doing and in knowing that she is doing the very best she can. That is what will distinguish her from Peg Bundy from the comedy series *Married With Children*. The same principle applies regardless of your career; be competent and always be the very best you can be.

2. We all have clients or customers in our lives. By definition, a client is someone who pays for or is in receipt of services or depends upon protection provided by another person. Be devoted to the best interests of your customer or client whoever they may be. We need to see customers, clients and everybody we deal with, as individuals and not just clients. For GM assembly line workers,

the customer is the one who will ultimately buy the car he/she is helping to construct. The children and their parents are the clients for the day-care provider, while the patrons at a hotel are the customers for the cleaning staff. There is always someone who is the beneficiary of our efforts and professionals always keep the customer's best interests in mind. I provide consultation as a means of generating income which, in turn, pays my bills. However, an integral part of this equation is that my efforts are ultimately in the best interest of the clients. If I engage in activities that are good for me but not for the client, in addition to making me short sighted, it means that I am not being professional.

3. Look after yourself and your responsibilities. If we fail to look after ourselves, we will be more likely to fail in our responsibilities to our clients. It is important that we strive to look after all aspects of our health—physical, mental, emotional and spiritual. It will help us to remain ever professional. To that end, a true professional will:

   • Get a proper amount of sleep each day. Contrary to what is portrayed about many types of interns (medical, legal and others), working 24 hours a day is never healthy and most certainly increases the odds and risks that mistakes will be made. Don't let that happen.

   • Eat and drink well. Proper nutrition and balance in what we consume can never be over emphasized. Learn everything you can about good dietary habits.

   • Exercise regularly but don't over-do it. Just stay reasonably fit. Keep active and busy; it is better than doing nothing at all.

   • Strike a good work/life balance—more about this in the next chapter.

   • Practise slow leadership, especially as a role model for others. So many people are trying to squeeze so much into their days that they forget how to enjoy quality in their lives. They try diligently to do too much in too little time. A slow leader is more likely to serve as a calming influence on others, achieving what needs to be done without undue rush and excitement.

4. A professional is always ethical. This is so important that I have dedicated an entire chapter to it later on. Briefly, being ethical means doing the right thing at the right time for the right reason. While at times we may justify misguided conduct by declaring it to be legally or technically correct, professionals usually have a very strong sense about what is right and what is wrong in a particular situation. Whether we follow "the Golden Rule" and treat others as we want and expect to be treated ourselves, or whether we have been brought up to follow the Ten Commandments (or the equivalent found in virtually every major religion), we generally know what is right and what is wrong. Mistakes may be made but our intentions must always be noble and ethical.

5. A professional will always demonstrate strong character traits, but what is the essence of "character"? Here are some of the qualities captured by that term:
    - Being honest (never lying or exaggerating the truth)
    - Being reliable (always following through on promises made)
    - Having a positive attitude
    - Being well-prepared
    - Being passionate about work
    - Being timely
    - Respecting others
    - Being courteous and well mannered
    - Trusting others and letting them know that they can always trust you

    Such a person can be an authentic leader for their staff, their colleagues, their family and their community. I can think of nothing more professionally or personally satisfying than knowing that all those I deal with trust me and believe that I always act fairly and reasonably.

6. Professionals communicate effectively and properly. Again, regardless of the field you are in, this is an important quality of being a professional. As such, there are certain practices that you need to follow:
    - First, avoid any airs in your conversation style. At the end of the day, remember that we are all just people so keep it

simple and avoid the overuse of jargon. Even those who are familiar with the jargon often tire of it.

- Second, always be honest but sensitive rather than brutally frank. Adopt a tactful and respectful conversation style.
- Third, pay attention when speaking with others. Multitasking by emailing or texting while supposedly listening to others just doesn't cut it. Make sure you truly listen when others are speaking.
- Fourth, try to personalize communication as much as possible by speaking to others one-on-one every chance you get. If not, use the phone with email/texting only as last resorts. Remember that email/texting seldom convey tone or body language, so a large part of every message risks being lost or misconstrued. The importance of effective communication for all leaders is discussed in a later chapter.

7. Be proud of who and what you are. Always represent yourself, your profession and your organization (even your family) with thought, care and dignity. I still meet with many who speak of themselves as "just a housewife" or "just the receptionist" or "only the Walmart greeter." It doesn't matter what you do because if your job wasn't important, it would soon be eliminated. When I met with the receptionist, referred to above, about her job, I had to point out to her that her face was the first one that visitors would see at the company and hers was the first voice callers would hear. From a public relations perspective, nothing could be more important than that first impression. She was not "just a receptionist" but a key part of the organization. A large part of Walmart's reputation hinges on their greeters, and there is nobody more important than mom or dad for all the little children out there who enjoy the benefits of having their parents stay at home with them. A professional should always be proud and, if for some reason you aren't proud of who you are or what you do, it may be time for a change.

8. One of the most basic tenets of being a professional is that you always spend time developing yourself and others. After all, isn't that the essence of true leadership as well? A leader, as I have

pointed out, is someone who inspires others, whether they are your children, your club members, your staff, your colleagues or your community. One way to inspire is by helping others grow and develop. However, improvement doesn't only apply to others. True professionals dedicate themselves to constantly developing their own knowledge and skills. They are akin to a sponge, always soaking up new information that will serve to make them better at their crafts and more capable leaders for others to follow.

9. No matter what your role in life or what your career is, never underestimate the value of building, nurturing and growing a network of relationships. We achieve very little in life by ourselves. There are other members of our team, those we lead, people we work with, clients and myriad other stakeholders who make our world go round. I can think of no better way to be successful in the community, at home or at any level of an organization than to build a network of positive, effective relationships. These, in turn, lead to opportunities to connect positively with others when we need help or when we are able to assist others. Remember, a person's wealth is not measured by material possessions but by the number of friends and associates whose company he/she enjoys. Build and maintain those relationships.

10. Professionals practice good emotional intelligence. This involves understanding and managing our own emotions, understanding other people as well as their emotions and managing our relationships with others. Emotional intelligence can be learned and developed. We're never too old to develop new skills and to change. Learn from your own experiences and mistakes as well as the experiences and mistakes of others.

11. Be prepared with all the right tools, equipment and clothes no matter what your role is, be it a banker, a plumber or a consultant. My father used to say, "There's no sense bein' poor and lookin' poor," and so it is with your appearance and being professional. Always appear like you know what you're doing. Dress appropriately for the job and always keep yourself clean and well groomed.

12. A true professional can be trusted with confidential information. Learn to keep your mouth shut and keep confidential matters

confidential. If you're going to share information about others, make sure it is the sharing of good information only. Also make sure that the other person wants it to be shared in the first place. There is no place for idle gossip in the world of any professional.

13. Finally, when I first wrote *Common Sense Leadership,* I had more than enough critics who asked, "Common sense isn't that common any more, is it?" There is nothing magical about common sense. Making it more common begins with each and every one of us. It doesn't come from book smarts but it does suggest that we all have an innate ability to apply solutions to problems that are simple to understand and even easier to implement. Common sense is logical and often follows what is "tried and true" without bowing to the whims of modern culture or media influences. It is something that, while hard to describe, is often so easy to apply. Things usually don't need to be as confusing as they seem to be and professionals know when to apply common sense to situations. Common sense leadership means, in part, keeping it simple and doing the little things well.

For all of us, engaging in these practices will convey a greater degree of professionalism regardless of your role at home, at work or in the community. And that just makes good common sense.

Principle #2

Enjoy What You Do

Regardless of what you do for a living and no matter what kind of leadership role you play, it is critical that you look forward to engaging in that role every day. As I noted in *Quit Your Job, Enjoy Your Work,* most of us will have neither the privilege nor the pleasure of being born into a life of abundant wealth nor will we become independently wealthy as a result of winning the next big lottery. As a result, the reality is that most of us will have to work full time for approximately 40 years of our life. We better enjoy whatever it is that we choose to do. Otherwise, it will become a waste of time for us and for our families.

In the last chapter I mentioned the importance of being the very best you can be at your chosen profession and approaching each day with a sense of adventure, optimism and enthusiasm. In my own career, I have tried diligently to look forward to each day and have prided myself in being the very best I can be. However, there have been times when I felt that I was losing my enthusiasm for a given position and, as a result, I would invariably move on to a new challenge. While I appreciate that not everyone can take on a new challenge that easily, the principle that is important to remember is that you may have to occasionally make changes in either your job or your approach to it in order to continue enjoying it day in and day out.

Occasionally, I hear from people is how much they love their job. In one instance, the individual mentioned that his job had its challenges and there were days that were certainly better and more fun than others but, on balance, he still loved his job after 40 years of service. That, to me, is priceless because when he is of that mind, he does his job better, his employer benefits and his family finds him a better person to be around. When we don't enjoy our jobs, nobody benefits. I have seen far too many individuals who come to work but are there in body only. Their mind and their spirit are somewhere else. For the balance of this chapter I will consider what we, as individuals, can do to make our jobs more enjoyable, and then I will finish with a look at what managers and employers can do on their part.

Enjoy What You Do

You must enjoy what you do. It is really quite immaterial what line of work you are in, or whether you work at home as a parent, run your own business or work for an employer of some kind. If you're not having fun, you need to make changes. I understand the attitude that some folks have that they simply cannot forego the great pay they receive or the benefits they are entitled to or even the pension they will eventually enjoy. I even understand that they may have dedicated much of their adult lives to developing the necessary skills, ability and education for their current job and, as a result, feel that turning back is not an option. However, I also firmly believe that to be stuck in a role that you are not happy with is not a healthy situation, nor is it worth the money and the benefits.

Life is too short to spend so much of it being unhappy. Forget what other people think or what they want. They don't have to be comfortable in your skin, but you do. As Will Rogers said, "Too many people spend money they haven't earned to buy things they don't need to impress people they don't like." The first and only person you have to please and impress is yourself. Others, including your parents, siblings, friends, neighbours and even your spouse and children will come later. If you don't look after you first, it will be a matter of time before your unhappiness will affect all of those relationships.

Assuming that you enjoy what you do then my next point is that it's okay to have fun at work while you are doing it. So how we can go about doing that? My father used to tell me that there is a time for work and a time for play. How could the two possibly be intertwined? Well, it remains my opinion that if you're not having fun while at work then there is something fundamentally wrong with you, your workplace or your organization and it is time for a change. But this doesn't just apply to you. The same applies to all of your staff. Many of us want our workplaces to be creative and energetic, filled with enthusiasm, fun and adventure. But isn't that what we want all aspects of our life to be, whether at work, at home or in the community? As I have noted, there are many who would have us believe that work is not meant to be fun but it is meant to be work and, for some reason, we need to keep the two separate and distinct. However, having fun at work does not mean that you become unproductive or unprofessional. As described by Gail Hahn, CEO of Fun*cilitators™ and author of *Hit Any Key to Energize Your Life*, the "fun" that I am talking about is "playful professionalism." If we recall what it takes to be a professional, there is nothing listed that says we can't have fun. We can still be competent, be devoted to our clients, be ethical, be passionate about our work and certainly be proud of who we are and what we do. Having fun takes nothing away from being professional, but it certainly allows us to enjoy what we do just a little bit more.

Attitude

Having fun and enjoying what you do is so often a matter of having the right attitude and the right approach to all things. We have all heard references to folks who see the glass as half full and those who see the glass as half empty. Which are you? Earlier in my career, I had the pleasure of going out to lunch on a weekly basis with a couple of my colleagues who, by and large, appeared to be fun loving and happy with life in general. To this day, I'm not sure why this happened, but every time we got together, they would tend to drone on about how rotten life was and what a sad state the world was in. After an hour of that sort of negativity, I would return to work feeling rather down and almost despondent. My glass was half empty and my mood invariably turned negative. Eventually, I stopped having lunch with them.

On the other hand, have you ever noticed that there are people who are just plain fun to be with and even if they aren't fun, they are always positive or make you feel better about life when you've spent a few minutes with them? In actual fact, I have hired individuals who perhaps were not as technically strong as other candidates but who were better suited for the team because I knew they would have a more positive influence on the rest of the team. In preparing for the writing of the original version of this book, one of the leaders I interviewed told me that "you can't train attitude." While I hold that to be true, there are things that all of us can do to make our world a more enjoyable place to be, whether that is at work or at home. In addition to making sure we enjoy what we do, having as much fun as possible and encouraging others to enjoy and have fun too, we can do the following:

- Focus on solutions, not problems
- Keep yourself and others positive
- Help people to laugh
- Keep everything in perspective

Focus on Solutions, Not Problems

When I was a young man, I had a boss who told me repeatedly, "Bring me solutions, not problems." In saying that, he was empowering me and encouraging me not to whine about issues but to see each problem simply as a challenge that needed to be met. If truth be told, life for each of us regularly puts problems in our path. It is never easy to make a job or career choice. In fact, I have often said, especially when engaged in job evaluation processes, that everybody sincerely believes that their job is tougher than everybody else's job. I have regularly heard comments like "You don't know how tough my job is" or "You should try it out here on the front line once in a while" or, my favourite, "Why don't you walk a day in my shoes?" In part, they are all right. Every job has its challenges.

There are many members of the public who believe that elementary school or high school teachers have something of an easy life with a nice 8:30 to 3:30 routine each day, weekends off, two weeks at Christmas, one week off at Easter and the whole summer off. What could be better? I am married to a retired school teacher, have a sister who is a retired school teacher and know a number of others who are in the field and, frankly, I wouldn't take their jobs for love or money. Most of them put in extra hours, can never please all of the children and parents (let alone the administration and politicians), have absolutely no power when it comes to appropriate discipline and, ultimately, are not appreciated for everything they do. There are those who would claim that staying home and looking after two or three kids would be fun—not for me! That's a really tough job.

One of the jobs I had as I worked my way through university was with a bumper manufacturer hoisting bumpers for seven or eight hours a shift. The pay was great. In fact, it was twice as much as anything else I could find at the time, but I couldn't stand the factory work, the dingy environment, the smell of the place or the boring nature of the work. When I quit and went to work for another employer for half the pay, there were those who looked at me like they could see water burning. For every job that you can imagine, they will have their problems and challenges.

There are very few jobs that one would consider to be perfect, but if the incumbent in any job were to focus on the problems, they would forget about all the good things that are part of their job. The bottom line is that we need to be positive about our jobs and our roles, whatever they may be, and we need to remember the good parts, finding ways to bring solutions to the problems as opposed to complaining about them. It's not easy but that's where our focus should be.

Keep Yourself and Others Positive

I know it's not easy to be positive every day of your life. Life is sometimes difficult for all of us but as leaders, if we are to inspire others (our family, our work colleagues and our community) if nothing else, our public persona should reflect an air of optimism. It will make you and everybody around you feel better. Ultimately, we all benefit. A number of years ago, when I had seasons' tickets for the Oshawa Generals Junior A hockey team, we had a team captain who apparently wasn't a "rah-rah" sort of guy, who inspired others by what he said. According to other players on the team, it was his "never give up" attitude that made all of them perform better, game in and game out. When he jumped on the ice, even if the team was down by three or four goals, he stayed positive and gave it his all. It didn't result in winning every game but it sure made a difference for every player on the team and, therefore, for the team as a whole. When the leader stays positive, it makes others positive too and, remember, we are all leaders in our own way. A friend recently shared with me the following essay by Charles Swindoll, simply called "Attitude":

> The longer I live, the more I realize the impact of attitude on life. Attitude, to me, is more important than facts. It is more important than the past, than education, than money, than circumstances, than failures, than successes, than what any other people think or say or do. It is more important than appearance, giftedness or skill. It will make or break a company . . . a church . . . a home. The remarkable thing is we have a choice every day regarding the attitude we will embrace for that day. We cannot change our past . . . we cannot change the inevitable. The only thing we can do is play on the one string we have, and that is our attitude. I am convinced that life is 10% what happens to me and 90% how I react to it. And so it is with you . . . we are in charge of our attitudes.[3]

Help People to Laugh

I know a manager who starts and ends each of his monthly meetings with a joke. While it sounds a little corny, for him, it works. It helps people to laugh and to relax, and I suspect we would all agree that a good laugh is healthy for you. Have you ever heard of anyone having a heart attack brought on by laughter? Not likely. Help people to laugh and while you're at it, laugh a lot yourself.

Do you remember when we were kids and laughter came so easily to us? Occasionally, on the television show *America's Favourite Home Videos,* you will see a very young child simply giggling. Anybody watching the video can't help but to start giggling themselves. It's infectious. Another view of laughter is found in *NUTS!* the nationwide bestseller about the zany antics at Southwest Airlines by Kevin and Jackie Freiberg. Here are a few of their tips that we can all use:

- Adopt a playful attitude. Go ahead and be silly, unconventional and find the humor in everyday work
- Think funny. It doesn't mean we don't take business seriously. We just find the funny parts of that seriousness.
- Be the first one to laugh. The worst thing that can happen is that everybody else laughs at you.
- Laugh with, not at. Don't find humor at someone else's expense but it is ok to laugh with them to help ease their day.
- Be prepared to laugh at yourself or as Ben Zander says, "Don't take yourself so damned seriously."
- Take yourself lightly but take your job and responsibilities seriously. [4]

Keep Everything in Perspective

It's up to every leader to remember what's important. Work occupies only a portion of our entire lives. When things become difficult and stressful, try to remember the things that are important not only to yourself but also to those around you. Will the issue be important six days from now? Six weeks? Six months? Is it worth losing sleep over? Should it be allowed to negatively impact your health or that of your loved ones or your relationships with others? Maintain perspective or simply consider the following story.

> A professor stood before his philosophy class and had some items in front of him—a large and empty mayonnaise jar, a bag of golf balls, a box of pebbles, a box of sand and two beers. When the class began, without speaking, he picked up the empty jar and filled it up with golf balls. He then asked

his students if they thought the jar was full and they agreed that it was. The professor then picked up a box of pebbles and poured them into the same jar and then lightly shook the jar. The pebbles rolled into the open areas around the golf balls. He then asked his students again whether they thought the jar was full and once again they agreed that it was. After hearing that, the professor picked up a box of sand and poured it into the jar. Naturally, the sand filled all the remaining spaces and once again, the students confirmed that the jar was full.

The professor then explained to the students that the jar is a representation of their lives. The golf balls are the important things such as their family, friends, health and other favourite passions. If everything else is lost, their lives would still be full with those items. The pebbles represented the other things that may be important such as homes, jobs, their cars, cottages, etc. The sand represented everything else or all the small stuff of their lives. If the sand were placed in the jar first, there would be no room for the truly important things in their lives. The key message was that they needed to pay particular attention to what was truly important and forget all the small stuff.

Just then, one of the students asked what the beers represented. The professor smiled and said that no matter how stressful life becomes, there is always time for a beer with a friend.

Keep things in perspective.

What Can Managers and Employers Do To Help Everyone Enjoy Work?

Up to this point I have focused on what each of us can, individually, do to enjoy our work. But I believe there is also a role for the managers and employers in helping staff to enjoy their work.

A Business Case for Enjoying Work?

Other than for the sake of simply having fun, is there any particular benefit to promoting the enjoyment of work? Can we build a case to support this?

The short answer is Yes!! Enjoying work is good for our health. It may help reduce absenteeism. It promotes employee engagement, making each of us more effective and efficient. And, it helps recruitment and retention initiatives. Let's look at each of these.

Enjoying Work Is Good for Our Health

Of course it is. Be selfish for a moment. If you're having fun at work, how does it feel? Great, doesn't it? Have a good healthy laugh and then look at yourself in the mirror. You are relaxed. You're smiling. You look great!! Undue stress adversely affects your entire body. Fun reduces stress. It's as good for you as a dose of cod liver oil, without "the yuck" factor. A good laugh increases blood flow which, in turn, promotes more effective functioning of all body parts. Those who have fun are more optimistic and, I believe, optimists generally live longer than pessimists and, even if they don't, they sure enjoy life more.

What about Absenteeism?

In this regard, I would invite readers to perform a simple study of your own organization.

Review the attendance records and history of various departments. I'm willing to bet that those divisions or departments that have the most fun also have the lowest absenteeism rates. While it may go beyond pure fun and focus equally on respecting and appreciating staff, the reality is that employees who are happiest attending work will have the best attendance records. We all have days when we don't feel 100 percent. If we aren't 100 percent healthy, a decision needs to be made about whether or not we go to work or call in sick. It may be a cold, a migraine or just a case of the 40oz. flu. If we feel respected, appreciated and an important part of the team and we generally have fun at work, we will show up. If not, we don't. We call the boss to say we can't make it.

Similarly, for a medical procedure, when our physician says we have to be "off work—four to six weeks," if we enjoy our work, we try to convince the doc that we're ready to go back after three weeks. If we don't enjoy our work, we try to negotiate a couple of extra weeks off. Add this sort of attitude up for the entire organization and having a fun workplace may just make a significant difference in the cost of your absenteeism rates. In my department in the last organization I was with, we had fun, we got along together well and there was a general sense of respect and appreciation for one another. Every year, we had one of the best attendance rates in the entire organization. While a solid work ethic may be one of the driving forces behind this success, I would respectfully submit that, more likely, it was the "fun" atmosphere that encouraged more regular attendance of all staff.

Are Staff More Engaged?

You bet they are!! Numerous studies have demonstrated unequivocally that there are immense benefits to organizations that promote employees having fun at work, the most obvious of which is that having fun or just being able to exercise a good sense of humour results in better performance, increased creativity, more productivity and an overall increase in job satisfaction. These employees, who are more engaged (i.e., they have more fun at work, enjoy their work, feel challenged, appreciated and respected) will suffer lower stress levels and enjoy more regular attendance. It is important enough that some more progressive organizations are starting to include some notion of having fun as one of their core values.

Turnover Is Decreased

If you can have fun at work and enjoy what you do, you are less likely to be interested in leaving your current employer in order to work elsewhere. While this may not be the only factor that affects staff turnover, it is certainly one of the major ones. Exit interviews that I have been part of over the years, with staff who have chosen to pursue opportunities elsewhere, clearly demonstrate that they almost never leave for more money or benefits. The clear majority of such terminations are the result of staff feeling unappreciated, disrespected or that the work atmosphere is simply unacceptable.

The Saratoga Institute, in 2005, conducted a study of 19,700 departing employees and discovered that 80 percent of those employees said they left because of poor relationships, poor development opportunities and poor coaching from the boss.[5] One of the biggest complaints heard from front-line managers was that staff recruitment activities took too long, did not produce guaranteed results and adversely affected the ongoing performance of the department. Experts project the cost of replacing staff to be—two to three times the annual salary of the position being filled. What on earth can we do about it? Keep your staff engaged, happy, enjoying what they do and having fun. If you do, you will dramatically increase the odds of retaining staff, reducing absenteeism, having a more productive staff and, at the end of the day, you and your staff will be less stressed and healthier.

Work/Life Balance

How many times have we all seen references to the importance of establishing a good work/life balance for ourselves and our staff? In a recent customer services review that I conducted, it came across loud and clear as one of the areas of concern that our department had to focus on for the future. In many, many interviews that I conducted in preparation for this book, managers shared with me their sense of the importance of work/life balance for their staff (though, admittedly, many did not practise what they preached, choosing instead to work huge amounts of overtime). They also emphasized that as leaders we need to establish reasonable expectations or else we risk losing too many staff to either ill health or turnover.

Often times, in order to address workload issues, staff may work through lunches, come in early, stay late or take work home. Technology, has made a 24/7 work routine far too convenient with work becoming too accessible and, far too often, the norm. In addition to workload issues, many staff face unrelenting personal stresses that may include child-care issues at home, spouses who are working double duty, elderly parents needing care, mortgage payments, medical appointments, pressure to stay fit (how do I squeeze that into my schedule?), and so on and so on. My God! Not only are we not having fun at work but we're killing ourselves by cramming too much into our lives generally.

So, what needs to be done? According to David Weiss and Vince Molinaro in their book *The Leadership Gap*, leaders need to apply the following:

1. Be a balance role model—practice what we preach, keep work hours and workload reasonable. Dedicate more time and energy to family and personal matters and be prepared to allow staff to do likewise.
2. Focus on what really matters—work is important but so is family and personal life. Focus too much on work and our personal lives suffer. When that suffers, work is bound to follow. Know your staff as individuals and accept that every staff member is likely facing personal challenges of some kind at home. They may be having marital concerns, problems with kids or parents, financial difficulties, health challenges for themselves or others, etc.
3. Adopt "slow leadership"—move away from the hectic, fast-paced life we normally "enjoy." Slow yields better conversations, better decisions, the right solutions to the right problems, and working at a more reasonable pace.
4. Sustain your personal energy—maintain proper levels of physical, mental and emotional fitness. Practice yoga, run, exercise regularly, take up meditation, read, go to church or whatever it takes to stay fit in all ways.
5. Grow a healthy support network—of friends, family, peers and colleagues. People that know and understand you will guide and support you and help you with work/life balance decisions.
6. Retreat—time off is regularly needed to slow down and contemplate what is really important. Enjoy weekends off and make sure you take regular vacations.[6]

In addition, there are actions that you can take to help ease the work/life balance for your staff. Consider any or all of the following:

- Be more flexible in work start and finish times. Understand that staff have personal challenges and issues that need to be addressed. Be flexible. Be understanding. Be compassionate.
- Compress work weeks. Other than collective agreement restrictions, can staff members work four 8 hour days instead of five 7 hour days? Why not? If the work still gets done and staff are happier, why should we care?
- Consider job sharing or part time positions. Two staff members can share one job for either a temporary period (to help raise kids, look after sick or dying relatives) or even on a permanent basis. Why do we always insist on full-time staff only? Not everybody necessarily wants or needs full-time work. Be flexible.
- Introduce telecommuting, virtual offices or work at home. While there are challenges with these programs and they may not be suitable for every job in the organization, keep an open mind for the possibilities. It doesn't have to be permanent or five days a week but, on an occasional basis, it can prove to be quite workable and beneficial for staff members who need the flexibility.
- Make sure that vacations are taken and enjoyed. Every year, in North America, thousands of employees fail to take allotted vacation time, choosing instead to carry it over or have it paid out in cash instead or sometimes, they just lose it. We all need to rest from time to time. We all need time off. Trust me when I say that none of us is indispensable. The work will be there when you get back and, usually, the company survives just fine in our absence. Take any time off that you are entitled to and preferably without taking the cell phone or laptop with you.

Making Work Fun

Some of these next ideas may work. Some may not. What are important are your attitude, your approach and the culture of your organization. Be creative and have fun with your staff and colleagues.

- Celebrate successes—have a cake—buy some donuts
- Go out for lunch or breakfast occasionally with your colleagues

- Harmless practical jokes are great but don't get carried away
- Dress-up days—don't be afraid to look silly
- Celebrate staff birthdays
- Decorate work stations; have a contest
- Set up hockey pools
- Sponsor contests that may connect with a corporate initiative such as health and safety
- Have a summer barbeque
- Enjoy a pizza party day
- Exchange gifts
- Celebrate baby showers or wedding showers
- Welcome new staff with coffee and donuts for everyone
- Get the gang together outside of work occasionally
- Have outdoor meetings in the good summer weather
- Do things that help keep the mood relaxed and fun

As we get older we sometimes appreciate the following sage counsel more than when we are young:

1. Throw out nonessential numbers. This includes age, weight and height. Let the doctors worry about them. That is why you pay "them."
2. Keep only cheerful friends. The grouches pull you down.
3. Keep learning. Learn more about the computer, crafts, gardening, whatever . . . never let the brain idle. "An idle mind is the devil's workshop." And the devil's name is Alzheimer's.
4. Enjoy the simple things.
5. Laugh often, long and loud. Laugh until you gasp for breath.
6. The tears happen. Endure, grieve and move on. The only person, who is with us our entire life, is ourselves. Be ALIVE while you are alive.
7. Surround yourself with what you love, whether it's family, pets, keepsakes, music, plants, hobbies or whatever else you like. Your home is your refuge.
8. Cherish your health. If it is good, preserve it. If it is unstable, improve it. If it is beyond what you can improve, get help.

9. Don't take guilt trips. Take a trip to the mall, even to the next county or to a foreign country but NOT to where the guilt is.
10. Tell the people you love, that you love them, at every opportunity.
11. AND ALWAYS REMEMBER: Life is not measured by the number of breaths we take but by the moments that take our breath away.

Principle # 3

The Niceness Factor

"A little bit of fragrance always clings to the
hand that gives you roses."

—Chinese Proverb

In the last chapter, I spoke of the importance of having fun at work or at least enjoying what you do. An extension of this notion of having fun is the need and importance of simply being nice to other people. For the life of me, I cannot understand what is so difficult about asking people to be nice to one another. But what does being nice really mean? It doesn't sound particularly profound. In fact, it should be quite simple. It involves some basic courtesies and the cementing of relationships in all aspects of our lives, at work, with our family and when connecting with others in our community. It also involves being sensitive to the wants, needs and challenges that others face. We are all part of the human race; no one person can be an island unto him/herself.

At work, none of us can achieve as much by ourselves as we can when we work collectively, as a team. If you are a manager, you need the staff who report to you if you hope to achieve your departmental goals. You can't do it alone. You need those at the same level as you in order for your organization as a whole to thrive. For your own piece of mind (and, in order to occasionally get what you want from them), you need to build solid relationships with your bosses and colleagues at the same level in the organization.

If you are an independent contractor, you may not have to worry about staff, bosses or colleagues. Being nice to clients and customers, real or potential, though, has immense benefits to the future success of your business. Even stay-at-home parents can realize value by simply being nice to others, especially if they ever need help with shopping, medical appointments, day care or occasional babysitting.

Building and maintaining relationships with all types of others is important to all of us in accomplishing our goals, in representing ourselves and our organization in a perpetual positive light and for the sake of pure enjoyment of life. Salespeople, suppliers, bureaucrats, politicians, family members and union representatives as well as a host of others occupy our time and energy and are entitled to our respect (although, clearly, they must first earn it).

I have spent years bargaining with union representatives. While I haven't always agreed with them or their positions on assorted matters, I have always found time to be pleasant, polite and respectful. If truth be known, I still golf regularly with a retired National Representative of the Canadian Union of Public Employees. Is that sleeping with the enemy? No. We have become friends and that started out as a matter of simple relationship building.

Regardless of the role played by anybody else, there are a number of measures and actions all of us can take to help build relationships. Let's look at some of these.

The Golden Rule

Let's start here. I have seen dozens of variations of The Golden Rule. For the purpose of this discussion, I shall define it as "Do unto others as you would have them do unto you." If we want others to be nice or pleasant or kind or courteous with us then we need to show them the same niceness, respect and courtesy on a daily basis. I once worked with a gentleman whose personal operating mantra was "I expect myself to be the first one in the office every morning and the last one to leave the office." What a leader! The only problem was that he was a miserable son-of-a-gun during the hours he was working. As a result, instead of being highly respected for his dedicated work ethic, he was reviled and generally loathed by those who worked with him.

That is just one example of someone I worked with who was not nice. I am sure that each of us has met or worked with someone that fit the same mould. If you want others to be nice to you, you need to be nice to them. The knife cuts both ways. Try for a no-exceptions policy in this regard. You'll be amazed at the results.

Good Manners

What should be common courtesy seems to have become more of a lost art. What happened to the good manners that our mothers and fathers taught us in our youth? Don't talk with your mouth full. Keep your elbows off the table. Say please and thank you. Hold the door for others. Respect your elders. And on it goes. It is immaterial where we work or what we do. I don't care how important we think we are, and I really don't care for those who are so preoccupied with their own thoughts and their own feelings of self-importance that they can't take time to say please and thank you to their staff, their colleagues or simply the person that serves them their coffee at the donut shop. It's an easy thing to do.

Even more impressive is taking the time to pass along a hand-written note of thanks or appreciation to a staff member or colleague. It's amazing how far that gesture will go in communicating to others just how "nice" you really are. Poor manners are inexcusable in any business, any culture and any relationship.

Relationship Building

When I said earlier that I had developed a solid relationship with a union rep that has now grown into a regular golf game, I should note that it was not the result of some magical connection between the two of us. Over the years, I routinely attempted to build relations with all union reps that

I dealt with, to learn something personal about each of them and find out what else was important in their lives. Did some of my colleagues frown on it? Absolutely. But did it result in my being able to build good relations with the unions? You bet it did. This principle also applies to your relations with your own staff, colleagues and significant others. The organizational leaders who are most successful and most respected by their staff and others generally are the ones who get to know their staff as individuals. They didn't necessarily set out to make new best friends but they did learn something about each one. They are not just human resources. As one person recently shared with me, "It's face time that counts." Don't hide in the office. Get out there and get to know your people.

I have been asked what the secret is to building good relations with municipal councillors. There is no magic. They are ordinary people who have ordinary lives. Some are brighter than others. Some are more eloquent or more down to earth or more energetic. They have values, beliefs and issues that are important to them. Try to discover who they are as individuals. Understand where they are coming from. If you are always pleasant to them, there is a good chance that they will respond in kind.

Just be prepared, for there are no guarantees. This applies to all relationships—there are still plenty of poorly mannered folks out there. Just don't stoop to their level.

Say Good Morning and Good Night

Many years ago, entertainer George Burns would close out his radio show with the words "Good Night Gracie," an expression of love to his late wife Gracie. What a nice way to end the show and, if you think about it, what a nice way to end each day. I recently spoke with a senior officer in a Police Service who shared with me that an exceptional way to move staff to follow you as leader is by simply saying "good morning and good night" to every member of your team. It is so simple yet so meaningful. It never ceases to amaze me that there are so many people in our world that have so much trouble simply saying hi, hello, good morning or good night (even a smile or a nod of acknowledgement is a major step forward for some). My goodness, there are some who can pass in the stairwells or in the hallways when you are the only two present and still manage to not look each other in the eye or to smile or say hello.

Don't expect your staff to be pleasant with each other or with your customers or colleagues if you can't make the effort to be pleasant yourself. Try it. Smile. Say good morning or good night as the case may be to everyone you pass. It doesn't hurt a bit. As a leader, you are not above this common courtesy, so don't ever fall into the trap of believing you are too important to acknowledge your staff or colleagues. I have tried to do this faithfully even in an organization of 4000+ staff members. In that case, it was impossible to remember all the names and faces but even if I didn't know their name or face, I still smiled and said hello. Everyone should do the same and it really doesn't require the passage of an organizational value or the issuance of a policy to make it work. Do it because it's the right thing to do, at work, at home and in the community.

Community Work

I sincerely believe that it behooves each of us to give back to our communities and, if we accept that we are all leaders, then that is one great way to inspire others. Every organization doing business in every community has a corporate social responsibility to give back to its community. In addition, as individuals, I believe all of us have a similar obligation.

Business enterprises are increasingly being expected to operate in an environment where the public can be assured of safe products and safe/healthy business practices. Consider the experiences of Johnson and Johnson and the Tylenol scare a number of years ago; Nike's response to charges of abusive labour practices in their factories abroad; lead found in toys manufactured in China recently; or the BP oil spill in the Gulf of Mexico (an environmental fiasco that resulted in the largest fine ever applied to a single corporation). In each of these cases and in hundreds of others, the public is demanding that leaders assure their stakeholders that workers are engaged in safe working environments and that the companies are promoting the proper use of limited natural resources, not contaminating the environment, reducing waste and maintaining ethical business practices.

These responsibilities are not limited to organizational CEOs. All of us have an obligation to give back to our communities in more ways than by simply paying our taxes. We can all show leadership by giving more to charity, by helping run organizations for kids, sitting on boards and commissions, volunteering at the local soup kitchen, helping the homeless, volunteering for our local senior citizens centre or any of a host of other initiatives. It may take a little extra time or money but, if we have it to give, everyone benefits. It is the sign of a true leader.

Gossip—Don't Do It

Another lesson learned from many of our mothers and fathers was "If you have nothing nice to say about someone, say nothing." It is as true today as it was 50 years ago. There is nothing so harmful or destructive to a person than to be the target of gossip or rumour. Don't listen to it. Don't engage in it and certainly don't pass it along when you hear it—and we have all heard it. Speak highly of your friends, family, colleagues, associates, staff and bosses and they, in turn, are more likely to speak highly of you.

I have been told that when people hear, secondhand, that you have said something positive about them, they find the news uplifting. However, when they hear bad things said about them, secondhand, they feel far more devastated than if they were to hear it firsthand. In my training sessions, I always try to finish with, "If you did not like today's session, please let me know. If you did like it, tell everybody else." Bad news or anything less than positive should be passed directly to the person who is the subject of that information. Don't tell anyone else. Gossip and rumours are great fodder for soap operas but have no value otherwise.

While I'm not sure it can be considered as "gossip", a current issue that has both positive and negative implications is the use of social media by so many members of the public. On the positive side, tools such as Facebook and Twitter have outstanding application as media for mass and instant communication. However, there are insufficient rules and guidelines relating to its use. As a result, there are many instances where reputations have been ruined, rightly or wrongly, in a flash. My advice in this regard is to exercise extreme caution in the information you post about yourself on social media, avoid discussing friends and colleagues online and never engage in posting damaging information or pictures of others. You never know where any of it will show up.

How Not to Judge Others

Diversity is one of the cornerstones of North American society. We are made up of all types of cultures, backgrounds, nationalities and orientations. In most organizations today, especially with the elimination of mandatory retirement, we have as many as four distinct generations in our workforce. It really doesn't matter what labels are applied to any group or individual. They all bring value to our lives and our organizations. Boomers are no better or worse than Gen-Xer's. White Anglo Saxon Protestants are no better or worse than any other race, creed or colour. We are all just people. It is best to judge others on the value they bring to their communities and their organizations. In some cases, there is a propensity to think that by tearing others down, we can increase our own feelings of self-esteem. In other instances, we often pass judgment based purely on first impressions such as tattoos, a different taste in clothing, body piercing, excess weight, a lisp, cell phone use, long hair, short hair, and so on. Wait until you know them before you judge them. Avoid taking a "holier than thou" attitude as you may find that you really aren't any better (or any worse) than those you have so quickly and easily passed judgment on.

Control Your Anger

I once thought there was some value to me getting angry on occasion. I felt that it somehow demonstrated leadership to others. However, I learned, far too late in the game, that all it ever does is lead to losing control and it usually brings about a loss of self-esteem, respect or appreciation. Even more important, it invariably deteriorates relationships. In addition, I cannot recall having made a good decision in a single incident when I was angry. In these moments, we do not think clearly and our anger serves no useful purpose.

If you feel yourself getting angry in any situation, walk away, cool down, calm down and go to Plan B. It will help dramatically if you recognize the signs that point to you losing your cool and becoming angry. Too often, anger just leads us back to the days of the schoolyard bullies. Don't be bullied, and don't allow yourself to get angry.

Reward and Recognition

Generally, when people think about reward and recognition, what comes to mind is official, organizational programs. Many organizations have programs that reward staff for serving faithfully for some designated length of time. (e.g., 5 years, 10 years). They may also have programs that recognize staff contributions that go above and beyond the call of duty. For example, showing exceptional initiative in cost cutting or inventing a new approach to streamline operations or making outstanding contributions to their community. While these types of programs are important, the one part which we can all contribute to and benefit from is simple day-to-day recognition. This is the part that all leaders can encourage and implement without being reliant on any official organizational program, and it is this part that relates to being nice.

As leaders, it is incumbent upon each and every one of us to foster a culture of recognition. You may not be able to influence the entire organization or the whole community but you certainly can exercise sufficient influence on your area of responsibility in order to make a difference in the lives of others. How do you do that? You're all leaders. Make sure you smile at work. Make sure your glass is half full. See your staff, colleagues and family as individuals—connect with them. Above all else, say thank you. Recognize them when they do something particularly well. But such thanks must be sincere and not overdone. I once had a boss who was a delightful gentleman but insisted on thanking me for everything I did. There were times when I think I could have committed manslaughter and he still would have thanked me for doing a good job of it.

Thanks are important and recognition for outstanding work or effort is critical, but it must be sincere and it must be appropriate in terms of degree, timing and situation (saying thank you in front of others, during a staff meeting, behind closed doors, in the hallway and so on). In one department that I had the pleasure of leading, we instituted a simple program called our Rays of Sunshine. This was created by the staff, not by me. Its intent was to encourage staff to give each other a note of appreciation when they caught colleagues doing something great (or just plain nice). It was continuously promoted by our staff recognition committee, which was departmental, not organizational, and resulted in hundreds of "rays" being given out. It generated interest and enthusiasm within the department and across the entire organization.

I know that this sort of thing doesn't work for every situation or in every organization but the principle behind it remains valid for all of us. Recognition of others is something we can all promote. It is easy, inexpensive, builds team spirit and contributes meaningfully to everyone's enjoyment on the job, at home and in the community. Best of all, it allows everybody the opportunity to just "be nice."

Leading and Being Nice By Serving Others

Servant leadership is a philosophy of leadership that promotes caring for the needs of others, being present when they need us most, being authentic and paying attention to people as individuals. There is more to it than this, but for the purposes of this discussion, what is particularly important is that leaders can be better at what they do by serving others rather than waiting for others to serve us. As I have noted previously, I am always reluctant to place labels on anything related to leadership practices or principles as it is far too easy to get caught up in terminology, definitions and jargon. What is really important is the behaviour that is followed on a consistent basis. This is called servant leadership.

Servant leadership is not a set of skills that we employ in the same way that management is a series of duties that we perform. Rather, it is a way of being and a way of conducting ourselves on a daily basis. It is an approach that results in the home or the workplace being far more enjoyable than it might otherwise be. Without going into detail about servant leadership, some of the aspects that are important for this discussion include the following:

- **Caring for others.** There are some who have a misguided notion that being a leader means that others can now look after us. However, the opposite is true in servant leadership. One of our roles is to ensure that we look after the needs of others. By doing so, we make them better and therefore better able to perform their roles and functions.
- **Being present when they need us most.** I am the first one to be critical of those who would micromanage their staff. However, being present does not mean micromanaging. It means that, as leaders, we are there to help and to serve when others need us most. It may be our staff, our families or our neighbours. It means not only being present but being ready, willing and able to provide support, advice and help.
- **Being authentic.** Lance Secretan has defined authenticity as being the perfect alignment of head, heart, mouth and feet with the result being that we are thinking, saying, feeling and doing the same thing consistently. Our actions always support the things we are saying, feeling and thinking. Ultimately, what is important is that the people we lead, live and work with come to trust us.
- **Being sensitive to the needs of others.** There are too many individuals in this world who are still primarily concerned about their own needs and not the needs of others. Servant leadership promotes a greater concern for the needs of those you deal with. Recognize other people as individuals who have problems and challenges to face. How can we understand them better and help them to overcome their difficulties?
- **Practice forgiveness.** I said earlier that getting angry is no answer to any situation. What is incredibly powerful, however, is the ability to forgive others when they harm to you. This doesn't mean that they have free reign to abuse you but, in the course of our lives, it occasionally happens that someone hurts us, intentionally

or otherwise. In these circumstances, servant leaders will always find it in their hearts to forgive most transgressions.

- **Build quality relationships.** This was noted earlier and the importance of having all types of solid relationships with friends, family, employees, bosses and others can never be overstated.
- **Help others to grow and develop.** This is obviously one of the key roles of a stay-at-home parent who must help nurture and guide children. Nothing is more important. However, it is also important for employees, managers and leaders at work and in the community to be ever prepared to help others to grow and develop. Like the orchestra conductor whose role is to make everybody else sound better, so it is with managers and community leaders. I often ask my audiences to reflect upon how they have made someone's life a little bit better each and every day. That is something we should all be striving to do.

Emotional Intelligence

A word needs to be said about the importance of emotional intelligence in our world these days. While IQ may tell us one thing about any person, EQ, or the measure of emotional intelligence, will often tell a totally different story. There are four parts to emotional intelligence and, for most of us, there is room for improvement in each of these areas.

1. **Self-awareness** is the ability to know ourselves and have a good, comfortable grasp of our feelings. It's okay to feel joy or sadness and its okay to let others know how you feel. We need to be comfortable in our own skin. We have strengths and weaknesses. It's important to know yours and what they mean for your potential to grow and develop, becoming the kind of person you truly want to be. Always maintain a good perspective on life and always live your life by a solid code of values.

2. **Self-management** relates to our ability to not only understand ourselves but also to do something with that understanding. Set goals for yourself and always strive to improve at every chance you get. You need to be at peace with your emotions but do not let

them get the better of you. Part of this self-management includes good work/life balance and the ability to enjoy personal renewal through good eating habits, sufficient rest and vacation time as well as regular exercise and continuous development.

3. **Social awareness** includes our ability to get along well with others—to just be nice. It refers to our degree of empathy and respect for others. We need to appreciate that everyone has personal issues, as well as emotions, strengths and weaknesses that we need to be aware of.

4. **Relationship management**, as I have noted, is a key feature of leadership for any of us. A high degree of emotional intelligence will result in stronger, more effective communications with others. It will also enhance team-building initiatives and promote the development and success of others.

In closing this chapter, I would like to share the following short story written by Kent Nerburn. It is called "The Cab Ride I'll Never Forget" and it communicates so effectively the positive affect that simply being nice to others can have on them.

> I arrived at the address and honked the horn. After waiting a few minutes I walked to the door and knocked . . .
>
> "Just a minute" answered a frail, elderly voice. I could hear something being dragged across the floor. After a long pause, the door opened. A small woman in her 90s stood before me. She was wearing a print dress and a pillbox hat with a veil pinned on it, like somebody out of a 1940s movie. By her side was a small nylon suitcase.
>
> The apartment looked as if no one had lived in it for years. All the furniture was covered with sheets. There were no clocks on the walls, no knickknacks or utensils on the counters. In the corner was a cardboard box filled with photos and glassware.
>
> "Would you carry my bag out to the car?" she asked. I took the suitcase to the cab and then returned to assist the woman.

She took my arm and we walked slowly toward the curb. She kept thanking me for my kindness. "It's nothing," I told her. "I just try to treat my passengers the way I would want my mother to be treated."

"Oh you're such a good boy," she said. When we got in the cab, she gave me an address and then asked, "Could we drive through downtown?"

"It's not the shortest way," I answered quickly.

"Oh, I don't mind," she said. "I'm in no hurry. I'm on my way to a hospice."

I looked in the rear-view mirror. Her eyes were glistening. "I don't have any family left," she continued in a soft voice. "The doctor says I don't have very long."

I quietly reached over and shut off the meter. "What route would you like me to take?" I asked. For the next two hours, we drove through the city. She showed me the building where she had once worked as an elevator operator. We drove through the neighborhood where she and her husband had lived when they were newlyweds. She had me pull up in front of a furniture warehouse that had once been a ballroom where she had gone dancing as a girl. Sometimes she'd ask me to slow in front of a particular building or corner and would sit staring into the darkness, saying nothing.

As the first hint of sun was creasing the horizon, she suddenly said, "I'm tired. Let's go now." We drove in silence to the address she had given me. It was a low building, like a small convalescent home, with a driveway that passed under a portico. Two orderlies came out to the cab as soon as we pulled up. They were solicitous and intent, watching her every move. They must have been expecting her.

I opened the trunk and took the small suitcase to the door. The woman was already seated in a wheelchair.

"How much do I owe you?" she asked, reaching into her purse.

"Nothing," I said.

"You have to make a living," she answered.

"There are other passengers," I responded.

Almost without thinking, I bent and gave her a hug. She held onto me tightly. "You gave an old woman a little moment of joy," she said. "Thank you."

There was nothing more to say. I squeezed her hand, then walked into the dim morning light. Behind me, a door shut. It was the sound of the closing of a life.

I didn't pick up any more passengers that shift. I drove aimlessly, lost in thought. For the rest of that day, I could hardly talk. What if that woman had gotten an angry driver or one who was impatient to end his shift? What if I had refused to take the run, or had honked once, then driven away? What if I had been in a foul mood and had refused to engage the woman in conversation? How many other moments like that had I missed or failed to grasp? We are so conditioned to think that our lives revolve around great moments. But great moments often catch us unawares. When that woman hugged me and said that I had brought her a moment of joy, it was possible to believe that I had been placed on earth for the sole purpose of providing her with that last ride.

I do not think that I have ever done anything in my life that was any more important. [7]

People may not remember exactly what you did or what you said, but they will always remember how you made them feel.

Remember to be nice to others, to have fun and to practice The Golden Rule. Always appreciate that almost everyone brings something positive into this world. Find every person's contribution and appreciate his/her value. It will pay dividends in the long run.

Principle #4

Always Act With Ethics and Integrity

"Dare to be yourself in the face of adversity. Choosing right over wrong, ethics over convenience . . . these are the choices that measure your life. Travel the path of integrity . . . for there is never the wrong time to do the right thing."

—Anonymous

A true leader will always follow my simple definition of integrity: he/she will always **do the right thing at the right time for the right reason.** As a friend and colleague once told me, "We all know the difference between right and wrong, but sometimes, it takes courage to do the right thing.". If you do nothing else after reading this book, remember this definition. It seems so simple, and yet we read and hear of transgressions on a daily basis. Here is a sampling of daily news stories about how people fail to apply an appropriate degree of integrity:

1. An employee is terminated for theft of organizational property, products or time.
2. Teachers or kids' coaches are found to be engaging in inappropriate sexual conduct.
3. It is revealed that certain athletes are taking performance-enhancing drugs.

4. Politicians are accused of abusing their position or power to satisfy some personal needs or gains.

5. Corporate CEOS bring their companies into disrepute by engaging in fraudulent activities.

It seems that nobody and no profession is exempt, and while that may sadden us somewhat, there is much that we can do as individuals to correct these situations.

First, let me note that the words *ethics* and *integrity* are used almost interchangeably by most folks. The distinction, in my mind, is that *ethics* refers to behavioural matters while *integrity* addresses consistency of behaviour. As a result, if we are ethical, we do the right thing at the right time for the right reason. If we have integrity, our behaviour in any situation can be counted on to be consistent with the values that guide that behaviour. We cannot allow ourselves to slip into a mode where we justify unethical conduct by saying "It's okay because he deserved it anyway" or "It's no big deal because everybody else does it too." There is always a morally correct way to do things and there are certainly morally incorrect ways of doing things as well. If nothing else, you can let your "conscience" be your guide.

So, how do we decide what constitutes ethical behaviour if there are no simple answers or measures? Some of the following guidelines may be helpful. For example, in *The Complete Guide to Ethics Management: An Ethics Toolkit for Managers*, McNamara identifies two broad areas of business ethics that we need to be concerned about. Although these guidelines focus on challenges faced by managers, they can easily be applied to all of us whether at work or at home or in the community:

1. **Managerial mischief:** In their book *Essentials of Business Ethics* (Penguin Books, 1990), Madsen and Shaftitz explain that "managerial mischief" includes "illegal, unethical, or questionable practices of individual managers or organizations, as well as the causes of such behaviours and remedies to eradicate them." There has been a great deal written about managerial mischief, leading many to believe that business ethics is merely a matter of preaching

the basics of what is right and wrong. More often though, business ethics is a matter of dealing with dilemmas that have no clear indication of what is right or wrong, an area referred to as moral mazes.

2. **Moral mazes:** This broad area of business ethics includes the numerous ethical problems that managers must deal with on a daily basis such as potential conflicts of interest, wrongful use of resources, mismanagement of contracts and agreements etc.[8]

While McNamara focuses his attention on the workplace, we all face situations where we may be tested by illegal, unethical or questionable practices. For example, when we are young we may be pressured by our peers to smoke or drink when we know this isn't the best choice for us. As adults, we are often pressured to having one more drink for the road when we know we shouldn't drink and drive? How many of us are involved in adulterous affairs? How many still cheat on our taxes? Drive too fast or break other traffic laws? Take office supplies from work for personal use or take unauthorized extended lunches? If we are in leadership positions, we are expected to conduct ourselves in legally and ethically correct ways. However, many of our challenges in life or the decisions we have to make do not fall into neat, black-and-white scenarios and, in many instances, we may not be sure of what to do. Regardless of our confusion at the time, it remains our responsibility to make wise and informed decisions that uphold our own integrity, as well as that of our families, our colleagues and our workplace.

The City of Toronto—The Bellamy Inquiry

In 2002, the Honourable Madame Justice Denise E. Bellamy conducted two inquiries dealing with questionable business and political practices at City Hall in Toronto. The Inquiry lasted three and a half years and involved 214 days of public hearings, 124,000 pages of documentation, 156 witnesses, 22 parties with official standing and more than 60 lawyers. The problems that were revealed are best explained by Madame Justice Bellamy who notes on pages 5 and 6 of her Executive Summary:

As the stories in this report will make very clear, people made mistakes. Some people disgraced themselves, failed in their duty to their City, lied, put self-interest first, or simply did not do their jobs. Many City processes and procedures were not up to the high standards that the people of Toronto have a right to expect. Some people did not show the leadership expected of them. Lines of responsibility and accountability were unclear or nonexistent. There was poor communication between people who should have been talking to one another and excessive communication between people who should have stayed at arms' length.

The Executive Summary is 108 pages long. The full report is a mammoth document, so suffice it to say that Justice Bellamy made 241 recommendations that would improve Codes of Conduct, hiring practices, training of staff and councillors, staff and council relations, conflicts of interest, complaints, investigations, lobbying activities and the hiring of a full time Integrity Commissioner.

While this particular case applied to a huge corporate entity, the ethics issues that were address by Justice Bellamy can be applied to smaller organizations as well as to all of us as individuals. She addresses our collective conduct, the importance of being leaders (and therefore inspiring others) and the importance of being accountable and responsible for our behaviour. That is the key.

In that regard, there are two levels of ethics that need to be considered. First, at an organizational level, regardless of size or number of staff affected, it is imperative that a program be established that achieves the following:

- Discourages conduct by staff that is illegal, may incur a reputational liability, harm the organization or violate any relevant policies.
- Ensures compliance with all legal and regulatory requirements as well as organizational policies and standards.
- Encourages a culture of ethical conduct and the promotion of an acceptance of questioning or challenging, as appropriate, decisions seen to be inconsistent with that culture.
- Delivers appropriate education to the entire organization.

- Addresses the managerial mischief and moral mazes as defined by by McNamara.

While we can collectively and corporately promote The Golden Rule (and, indeed, it would be a noble goal to strive for), we will experience constant attempts to undermine our goals, especially those of us who are in positions of power. Pressure will be applied by vendors, developers, friends, family, neighbours, political constituents and others who are seeking business opportunities, jobs, concessions, deals and favours. In these situations, we may find ourselves being tempted with drinks, food, golf, gifts and so on.

This is where the the second level of ethics comes into play. The second level requires that each one of us be responsible for ourselves and our decisions. While we should follow The Golden Rule as well as our personal values, we must also follow our organizational policies, values, practices and culture in making our decisions.

Michael Josephson, in *The Six Pillars of Character*, identified six core values and principles that are an integral part of the development of our own ethical code of conduct and should be a critical part of our organizational culture and value system:

1. **Trustworthiness** includes being ethical while demonstrating honesty, reliability and loyalty. It means demonstrating integrity in our decision making and being true to established organizational and personal values, principles and practices. It encourages us to avoid bad faith excuses or unwise and unclear commitments. If we want a reputation of being trustworthy, it is critical that our behaviour, at all times, reflects truthfulness, sincerity and candor.
2. **Respect** includes respecting ourselves and others. Respect encompasses the need to respect all people regardless of race, creed, colour or other distinguishing features. It means not allowing ourselves to engage in intimidation or coercion of others, but to promote others' autonomy and avoid excessive discipline.
3. **Responsibility** means being accountable for our actions and decisions and being responsible for pursuing excellence in all that

we do. As leaders, it means we lead by example, are reliable, exercise self-control and perpetually focus on improving ourselves.

4. **Fairness and transparency** mean that we always settle disputes or divide/assign resources equitably and that we do not show favouritism or prejudice. As well, we are expected to quickly and effectively correct mistakes or injustices affecting others when we have the power to do so.

5. **Caring** and being genuinely concerned for the welfare of others includes being generous with our time, energy and money.

6. **Citizenship** prescribes how we behave as part of a larger community of people. We must know and obey the laws of the land. In addition, we should be aware of the issues of the day, be concerned about our environment, volunteer our time and do our part to make society function in better ways.[9]

It should be noted that some of these values have already been captured in earlier chapters that are dedicated to being a professional or being nice to others. This duplication is intended to show that these values are also a key part of the discussion on ethical behaviour.

Organizational Ethics

Remember, organizationally, we want to ensure that our collective conduct:

- Does not constitute action that can ever be considered to be illegal
- Will not incur any liability for the organizational reputation
- Is consistent with the organization's values, policies and standards

Therefore, for those leaders employed in larger organizations, what is needed is a single, comprehensive ethics policy/program (which includes elements of effective communication, education and complaint investigation/resolution), a well thought out slate of values and a leadership team that is prepared to walk the talk and is obsessed with fairness. This is not to say that having a policy or program in place will guarantee that everyone will abide by it. What it will provide is an ethical beacon for all staff to follow. For those who work in smaller organizations, from home or as independent contractors, you may not have a written policy or program but these principles are sound and will apply nonetheless.

Policy/Program

Many organizations have any or all of the following policies: code of ethics, harassment and discrimination, conduct and behaviour, conflict resolution, conflict of interest and confidentiality. Many may also have an assortment of related procedures and practices that may, unfortunately, confuse staff rather than guide or enlighten them. These corporate initiatives should go hand in hand with other policies that are intended to prevent cases of "managerial mischief." The purchasing department will have its policies, while HR will craft hiring practices and finance will establish risk management programs. These are examples of policies and practices intended to guide staff and ensure that their behaviour and conduct is as honourable and morally correct as possible.

However, this collection of well-intended initiatives should be cast aside to make room for one comprehensive ethics program that includes guidelines for all staff, from management to entry-level workers: communication strategies, educational programs and a process for the filing, investigation and adjudication of complaints. The program cannot be a one-time initiative as many organizations seem to believe. Many organizations create an ethics program and then pat themselves on the back for having done a marvellous job, all the while forgetting that managing ethics is an ongoing process. The spirit and intent of the ethics program is to promote preferred behaviour and to be proactive in facing potential problems. It needs to be engrained in the very fabric of the organization as another management practice that all staff are aware of, promote and support. It cannot be just "one of those HR things." To that end, the following points represent the key components of a comprehensive ethics program for an organization.

Values

Every organization (and, in fact, every person) should have four or five core values that become integrated into each and every one of its business activities. These values not only guide staff in their day-to-day conduct but also aid them in making all organizational decisions. The values should not be elaborate or cumbersome; instead, they should be easily memorized, recognized and referred to by all staff and key stakeholders. They cannot be seen simply as nice words found in the Annual Report or posted at the main entrance to the headquarters. They must be integrated into the ethos of the organization.

Leadership Must Walk the Talk

This is one of the most important characteristics for all organizational leaders and, in fact, all leaders at home and in the community. It serves no useful purpose whatsoever if any of us, as leaders, talk about ethics, fairness and respect yet conduct ourselves in a totally different fashion. It will ultimately become counterproductive. You can't have one set of rules for some and something different for the leadership. "Do as I say, not as I do" simply does not cut it in this day and age. Leadership decisions and actions must reflect organizational values, and their personal values should align with those organizational values as well.

Leaders would be well advised to regularly remind themselves and others of the existence, content, spirit and intent of the ethics program. A simple example of how this can be done is to include a discussion of the program as part of every performance review. That discussion may be at a philosophical level, or it may only examine how each employee feels the organization is doing on the ethical front, or it may drill down a little deeper to consider how an employee has demonstrated adherence to the organizational values in his/her behaviour and conduct over the last year. If nothing else, it forces people to at least have the discussion and brings the topic of organizational values to the forefront of their thinking.

Individual Ethical Conduct

One of the things that is of primary importance for me in writing this book is that I give some guidance as to how you can become better leaders, regardless of the environment you work or function in. Two ways of doing this are to consistently make decisions that are ethically correct and, to every extent possible, do the right thing at the right time for the right reason. Whether we are employed in major organizations, own our own business, or work as union leaders, politicians, service club members or stay-at-home parents, as individuals, we must always act ethically.

I have made it clear that I believe every organization should have a comprehensive ethics program. If your organization has one, become familiar with it and review it occasionally. It is important that all staff and the organization as a whole believe in and promote the ethics program. Managers must support it wholeheartedly and expect their staff to follow it to the letter. Notwithstanding this support, it is not always easy to determine ethical conduct and the rightness or wrongness of any particular action. If in doubt, it is always wise to get a second opinion from someone else you trust in the organization.

If your organization does not have an established ethics program, there is nothing stopping you from creating your own personal or departmental code as a way to protect everyone against claims of unethical behaviour. Establish a code of conduct, create policies and practices regarding confidentiality, conflicts of interest or protection against workplace intimidation, harassment or other discriminatory activities. All staff will appreciate the effort and your professional dedication to higher ethical standards. If any of your colleagues fail to demonstrate high ethical standards once they understand what is expected of them, it becomes questionable whether or not they should remain a part of the team.

For those who are not part of a larger organizational context, the principles remain sound. We all need to live by certain values and conduct ourselves on a daily basis in accordance with those values. In many of my workshops, I share a list of 50 or so values and ask participants to select the 10 that they believe most accurately reflect their personal values. When they have done so (and sometimes it is difficult for them), I ask them to take their list of 10 and reduce it to 5. This ensures that their core personal values have been well thought out and are truly reflective of what is important to them. Can you imagine how it might affect the world if each and every one of us were to commit to living our lives in accordance with a key set of values? It wouldn't matter if we all have the same values. It would certainly increase the odds that the world, as a whole, would be the benefactor and would make for a far more ethical place to live, work and play.

Decision-Making Tests

There are a multitude of approaches any of us can take when facing difficult decisions, especially when ethical conduct is part of the equation. Some of the considerations that we may use to arrive at a sound and ethical decision include:

1. The Golden Rule: This rule was referred to earlier and it stresses the importance of doing unto others as you would have them do unto you. If somebody else were making the decision you are now contemplating and it directly affected you, how would you feel about the final decision? Can you respect it? Is it ethical? Is it the right thing to do for the right reason at the right time?

2. Disclosure: If you take a certain action, will you be comfortable if all your friends, associates and family members are aware that you have done so? Would you be proud or it or would you be more inclined to hide your face if it became known what you decided to do?

3. Intuition: Not very scientific but what does your "gut" tell you to do? Will the decision allow you to sleep at night or will it keep you up?

4. The categorical imperative: Can the principles that you apply to an action or decision be adopted by everyone or will it force you to tell others to "do as I say and not as I do"? If I intentionally cheat on my taxes, is it okay to allow everyone else to do likewise? If I take a pad of company paper for personal use, is it all right if my

staff were to do the same thing? Can I offer a friend a job but not support my staff who want me to offer their friend a job as well?

5. The professional ethic: Could you support your decision if the issue came before a committee of your peers?

6. The Utilitarian Principle: If in doubt, a decision should do the greatest good for the greatest number of people. Who gets their road ploughed first in a winter storm? Those with the most money? The squeaky wheel? Councillors? The roads that get the most usage regardless of who lives there? Which would you choose? What is the ethically correct decision?

7. The Newspaper Consideration: Would I be comfortable if my action/decision were to appear on the front page of a major newspaper? If I am worried for reasons other than the sheer publicity, perhaps my decision needs to be reconsidered.

8. A Source of Pride: Is this a decision that will bring pride to me, my family, my community or my organization? For many of us, we also need to consider whether or not it would bring pride to our parents.

9. Consistency: Is the decision consistent with our organizational or even my personal values or code of conduct? Those values are there to guide me so I need to be certain that I regularly reflect on them.

Expectations of Others

Leaders at all levels, whether it be at home, in the community or in a large or small organization, must exhibit characteristics such as respect for others, trustworthiness, authenticity and sincerity. These are the characteristics that staff, friends, family, neighbors and others appreciate and respect in their leaders. However, here are some others that are also important and that can benefit all of us if we simply use them:

- Walk the talk (already discussed at length)
- Encourage best practices from ourselves, our areas of responsibility, our staff, our families and our community colleagues
- Be consistent in our thinking, speaking, feeling and acting

- Always be fair with others
- Be sensitive to others and always compassionate
- Be reliable
- Exercise self-control and always remain calm
- Avoid assigning blame

Remember, all you can ever truly control is your own behaviour and the spirit, intent and actual way in which you carry out your decisions. Make sure you walk the talk, promote ethical behaviour in others and never be afraid to ask yourself if this is the right thing to do for the right reason at the right time. Pure ethical behaviour is an ideal to be aimed for, although it sometimes appears elusive. Keep practicing and keep aspiring to be the best person you can possibly be.

Principle #5

Respect Time

A man with a watch knows what time it is. A man with two watches isn't quite sure.

A tourist in Italy had left the hotel without his watch. Not knowing what time it was, he stopped a peasant with a donkey to ask the time. The peasant lifted the donkey's tail and said, "It is 9:15." While he was unsure how the man told the time by lifting the donkey's tail, the tourist nonetheless thanked the peasant and went on his way. A short while later, the tourist once again came upon the peasant and once again asked what time it was. The peasant lifted the donkey's tail and said, "It is 11:30." This time the tourist could not contain his curiosity and asked, "How can you tell the time by lifting the donkey's tail?" The peasant invited the tourist to bend over and he himself could lift the donkey's tail. The tourist did so and when he did, the peasant asked, "Now, can you see the village clock on the other side of the donkey?"

While it can be said (and it often is) that there are only two things that are certain in life, those things being death and taxes, there is also a third certainty: time. Each and every one of us, in every week of our lives, no matter what our race, creed, colour, sex, job, wealth or social standing, shares the same amount of time: we each have 60 seconds in every minute; 60 minutes in every hour; 24 hours in every day; and 168 hours in every week. All too often we fail to respect the fact that time is a limited resource both for ourselves and for everyone else. My rule in this regard is simple:

"respect time and don't be late for anything." In every new job I have taken over the last 30 years, I have met with the staff of my department and indicated *on day one* that I have only two rules. First, I expect us to act as a team, perhaps disagreeing on occasion but always behind closed doors and regardless of any disagreements, we always, when in public, support one another and work as a team. (This is the topic of a future chapter.) Two, I expect my staff and everybody they work with to be on time. Not everyone fully appreciates this rule. I consider it to be common sense and common courtesy. Some folks show up late for meetings because they "just had a couple of things to do before coming down" or they "had to make or take one more phone call" or "Bob dropped in unannounced." Often, when you travel a distance for a meeting, it seems to me that the one participant who lives the closest is the one who is always late.

A former boss of mine was a true gentleman but he had a terrible habit, and the reputation to go with it, of being late for everything. In fact, as I often told him, I feared he would be late for his own funeral. After a while, it was no longer a joke. His lateness became downright disrespectful. What possesses people to **not** be on time and what can be done about it? What are typical time wasters and what are some of the more contemporary issues that we face?

Why Are Some People Not Timely?

I'm not sure that there is a simple answer to this. It could be that some people just don't care. Make sure that this is not the case for you. If you know someone you suspect doesn't care about punctuality, bring it to their attention. As I noted previously, to be late for appointments or meetings with anyone is simply disrespectful and a huge time waster. Don't do it and don't allow yourself to be a victim for somebody else.

In all honesty, I don't believe most people who are routinely late fall into the category of those who don't care. A more likely scenario is that they have little self-respect or no respect for others or simply have no appreciation for how important time really is.

Another possibility is that some people, according to writers such as Stephen R. Covey in *The 7 Habits of Highly Effective People*, just have trouble setting priorities. As such, it is not so much a matter of managing time as it is of managing ourselves. The activities that we engage in on a daily basis are many and varied, regardless of our career, status or position. A stay-at-home parent may deal with household chores, kids, schools, the medical community, pets, their own parents, shopping, personal needs and a host of miscellaneous other chores and functions. In order to able to achieve anything positive during the day, he/she will need to get organized, determine which activities are urgent, which ones are just important and which ones are of no particular consequence. Washing the car may be something that we would like to get done but if it results in the kids being late for school or missing medical appointments, then the time has truly been wasted.

Although perhaps of a different magnitude, the responsibilities and functions of the company president are not really that different. He/she still must determine what is of critical importance, perhaps for the very survival of the company, and which chores can be set aside or are simply less important. The reality is that we all need to organize ourselves such that we are able to achieve the most important things most of the time.

If you are regularly late for meetings or appointments, then there is a good possibility that you are spending too much time on less urgent or unimportant activities and not dedicating or disciplining yourself to set priorities. As a result, though we may know that we are expected at an appointment by a certain time, we allow others to interfere with our schedule or we allow interruptions or we get sidetracked and, ultimately, arrive late. We need to set priorities and effectively plan our day.

How Do We Do a Better Job of Managing Our Time?

As I noted just above, we each have so much time that is given to us each and every day. It is not a renewable resource. We have no ability to save some of our time for a rainy day. As a result, if we don't use our time productively, we can be certain that we will suffer tremendous stress and frustration and, beyond a doubt, we most likely will not inspire anybody. None of this is intended to suggest that we have to account for every minute of every day in what might be considered a productive fashion. We can always take a few moments to enjoy ourselves, our lives, our friends and our families. But, in the meantime, as leaders, we must use most of our time effectively. How can we do that? The following nine tips can help.

Be Aware of Time

There is no magic to this tip. It is a matter of discipline and being aware of where you are supposed to be and at what time. Knowing that being late is inconsiderate and disrespectful of other people and their schedules, we can all discipline ourselves to abide by a "no-exceptions" policy when it comes to being on time. No interruptions. No allowances for "just one quick question." No last-minute phone calls and no blaming the weather, traffic or other circumstances generally considered to be beyond our control. Give yourself plenty of time and be there—ON TIME!!

There is no excuse to be "fashionably late." We see it too often in our business lives and in our personal lives. I can never understand why a doctor's office, for instance, makes an appointment for me at 9:00 a.m. and then the doctor is routinely late in seeing me. A doctor's pay should be docked for every minute I am kept waiting. Doctors either do a poor job of scheduling or they just don't care. Either way, it is unacceptable. I understand the need to book appointments back to back in order to get the most mileage out of your schedule, but don't book them so tightly that they disrupt the schedules of your patients. And doctors aren't the only offenders. This cuts both ways. If I have an appointment for 9:00 a.m. on a wintry morning and I know it takes me 15 minutes on a sunny Sunday afternoon to get to the office, then on that snowy traffic-clogged Monday morning, I should allow extra time to get there, get parked and get into the office.

Collectively, we need to be more aware of time and respectful of others. In short, we need to be disciplined.

Wherever You Are, Be There in Body, Mind and Spirit

When I was growing up in the 1950s and 1960s, it was certainly a different world. My dad worked and my mom stayed at home to look after six kids and my grandmother. For the most part, Dad did not have to worry about what was going on at the home front. Things were being looked after. Today, it is a vastly different world. Not only is the family unit often different in its makeup but, in the majority of cases, both parents have to work just to make ends meet. They have kids to worry about and, in many cases, parents and perhaps grandparents. They may be facing financial concerns, problems with the house or the neighbours, health challenges, legal questions to be answered and so forth. As a result, many of us are inadvertently thinking about personal problems when we are at work as well as bringing work problems home with us. The result is that these distractions often make us less productive and less focused than we may otherwise be.

Again, self-discipline is the key, but that may be easier said than done. Some suggest that we focus on work in 20-minute bursts followed by a brief pause to contemplate pressing personal matters. It may not work for everyone, but what is important is that you establish your own system for separating work thinking from personal thinking. As an employer, as a manager or even as a parent or member of the community, you must be prepared. This issue regularly crops up. Again, addressing these distractions requires discipline. Be aware of time and stay focused on all matters that require your attention. It will allow you to utilize your time more effectively.

Prioritize Your Activities

Again, everyone has their own way to do this, whether it by keeping to-do lists, maintaining daily or weekly calendars or even writing notes and sticking them on your desk. Everyone has their own system. Whatever your approach, it is important to remember to use your time wisely. Spending time on activities that are not important will serve to derive no net gains whatsoever. Move the most important activities to the top of your list and address them first.

But, be aware! Make sure you know and fully appreciate what it is that makes an activity important or unimportant. Evaluate carefully. For example, destroying a good personal or business relationship in order to finalize some other task may not represent a sound system of prioritization. My first suggestion is that you establish goals at the beginning of each and every day/week/month/year. What is it that you hope to accomplish at the end of the period in question? Next, keep the goals reasonable. There is no real need to achieve everything possible during the course of any day. I still know far too many good people who try to squeeze every ounce of life out of every minute of every day available. The result is they are often tired, run down and really don't achieve as much as they would like or as much as they might otherwise achieve. Slow leadership is the key. Take time during the day to look at what you hoped to accomplish (if you need to, write your goals down somewhere). It serves to refocus your energy and allows you to use the time more effectively. Always be sure to know the value of what you want to accomplish so that you can achieve those goals that generate the most value first.

Shut The Door!

I usually offer this advice to managers in the workplace but it applies equally to those at home and in community organizations. I'm the first one to promote an open-door policy, which is an approach practised and encouraged by most of our better managers and leaders. However, on occasion, it is more than acceptable for any one of us to shut the door, turn off the phone and/or computer and not allow any interruptions or distractions. This sort of tactic should not be used indiscriminately, but it can be an effective tool if used on occasion. Similarly, technology allows us, at home or at work, to let phone calls go to voice mail if our priority is to meet a deadline, get the kids to school or make it to a medical appointment on time. We can call back later when time allows. Don't try to squeeze in one more call, one more email or one more meeting before taking care of what is important. Stay focused. Figuratively speaking, shut the door.

Handle Chores/Paper Only Once

Too often, we receive memos, reports, letters, bills or other correspondence that we examine and then set it aside to deal with later. Most of us have an occasional tendency to procrastinate or even simply defer decisions until some future point in time when we are somehow better prepared. The only result that comes of this procrastination is that we handle these materials more than once, thereby duplicating our efforts and wasting precious time. When you receive bills, memos and so on, deal with them as soon as possible. Bear in mind that, on occasion, after reading a piece of mail, you may determine that more information or research is necessary before you can take action. That's okay. Don't take the suggestion to handle things only once too literally. But, if you can save some time this way, you will be the ultimate benefactor.

Save Up the Discussions

Most of us, in our daily work, have a number of people with whom we maintain regular contact. Instead of calling, emailing or visiting with them for each issue as it arises, why not save up a list of items to discuss and try to meet less regularly. It is less time consuming but still allows us to maintain that all important personal relationship and, in fact, reduces the use of email and creates a personal, more time effective touch.

Be More Selective About Your Professional Readings

If you receive innumerable professional articles and journals (or, for that matter, this applies to the newspaper, junk mail and magazines) on a daily basis the way I do, you may want to choose not to read them during the busiest time of your day. Be more selective about what you read and when you read it. Read the ones that are truly valuable in your quiet time on the train, at home, over lunch or before your work day officially starts. You may find it more relaxing and you may just get more out of the reading.

It's Okay To Take A Break

Going through and simply surviving each day may occasionally feel like we are working our way through a marathon or some other kind of endurance test. However, unlike marathons, we will be more productive and generally function better if we take the odd break during the course of the day. Like our annual vacation or even the days off that we earn and enjoy each week (for all but the stay-at-home parent who, for the most part, doesn't have a day off), taking breaks during the day will regenerate our brains and our bodies so we can properly complete all the tasks we have set out for ourselves. Our bodies are not meant to work at a high pace for 24 hours a day. We need to have the opportunity to stop occasionally. Don't look at these breaks as "wasting time." They are important bits of downtime which serve to keep the body, mind and spirit functioning more creatively and effectively. They don't need to be long but long enough for a quick walk, a cup of coffee or to simply relax or meditate wherever you are. Also, make sure you take appropriate and regular meal breaks. There is nothing more valuable than maintaining a proper diet. Skipping meals will not make you more productive but leave you feeling even more fatigued. Regular meals, even snacks, can help you re-energize. They're not a waste of time.

Don't Take On Too Much

I know, for some of us, it's difficult to say "No" to various requests for assistance. You don't need to be Superman for everybody at work or SuperMom while at home. Taking on too many projects, jobs or commitments often leads to nothing more than doing a poor job on all of them. The first thing that needs to be done is to ask yourself these key questions: Why am I taking on so much? Is it because that is the nature of my personality or is it because I have a big "sucker" stamped on my forehead and I end up doing everybody else's work for them? Am I perhaps a micromanager? If I am then it means that there are two people busy doing one job. If that's the case, one of us isn't needed!!

If taking on too much is a by-product of your essential personality, then perhaps it is time to learn to effectively say "no" to additional tasks and learning how to do it in a way that allows you to maintain a good relationship with the person you are declining. Stopping the habit of being a micromanager is not only in your best interests but will also empower your staff, and they certainly will appreciate it. Learn to trust them and if they can't be trusted to do their job, you need to consider whether or not they should stay employed with you. Perhaps it is time to allow another employer the opportunity to enjoy the skills, abilities and talents of that particular employee.

New Issues

There are a number of new issues that are increasingly evident today that were non-issues 20 or 30 years ago. I want to discuss three of them.

First, as was noted earlier, we are seeing a shift in family life in which both parents have to work, and which places the care of family members on many of us who have to look after not only our own children but also our elderly relatives. As workers, we face demands on the home front and on the job. We have bills to pay, chores to perform, appointments to keep and a relentless pressure to stay educated as well as fit and healthy. There are not enough hours in the day. We need to be aware of stress and burnout. The advent of computerization and technology has been something of a double-edged sword. It can certainly be a problem as has been noted repeatedly in this book as there is a clear tendency for many workers to work longer hours and accomplish more than ever before. However, it must be remembered that it might allow some employees to attend to family issues, education, healthcare appointments and so on during normal work hours and finish work at times that are more suitable to their own life and schedule. This may serve to improve the work/life balance for many, yet mark the end of the 9-to-5 work schedule for others. Flexible working arrangements—including flexible working hours, alternative scheduling, telework and job sharing—are becoming increasingly more the norm for many. It won't work for all staff and all jobs, but it is becoming more prevalent.

Second, one thing my dad never had to worry about and neither did I for most of my working life is the reality that, in these days, information is instantly available through the internet. This is wonderful news when you are looking for that information but it also means that others may make requests of each of us and their expectations of us are such that we feel pressure to respond accurately and immediately to a host of work demands. This is aided and abetted by the advent of cell phones, home computers and other technology that allows bosses, staff, customers and others to track us down instantly and on a 24/7 basis. While convenient, it is not an acceptable practice to routinely engage in. Too many staff are now taking their equipment and communication devices on vacation, to the restaurant, to the movies and elsewhere, answering messages every weekend and even when off work recovering from illness or surgery. We must find a better balance and achieve better time management skills. There is work time and there is personal time. While the distinction between the two has become blurred, we must collectively guard against flagrant abuses. It is especially important that those who are acting as organizational or community leaders recognize this tendency and ensure that they don't place unrealistic demands on their staff or colleagues and that all of us, for our part, don't allow ourselves to fall into this unnecessary trap. Surely, we can do a better job of managing and respecting our time and the time of others.

Third is the overuse of email. How many emails do each of us receive during what might be an already harried workday that we need to read and possibly deal with? When all is said and done, we so often shake our heads and say to ourselves, "What on earth did that have to do with me?" Ultimately, there was no need to receive it, to even know about it and certainly not to waste time reading it or dealing with it. Group distribution lists are great for this sort of time-waster. At one point in the not-too-distant past, I was the chair of an organization that belonged to a larger provincial organization. For a long time, I was included on a provincial distribution list for information that seldom applied to me or the organization that I represented and was of no interest whatsoever. However, each time I received one, I would read it and try to decide what to do with it. I ultimately recognized these messages as time-wasters and started deleting them (which still took too much time) as they arrived. Other group messages tell us about cars in the parking lot with their lights left on, keys found in the stairwell, an upcoming professional conference or just the act of being copied on issues that we don't need to be copied on—great time-wasters!! Beware of them as they are becoming increasingly common in today's world.

Speaking of time-wasters, here are a few others:

Meetings—How many of us, who are expected to attend meetings on a regular basis, have rolled our eyes or sighed in pain at the thought of (sometimes, we even do this during) another painful, wasteful, frustrating meeting? A number of things can make meetings unnecessarily difficult: an agenda that is not followed, a meeting that doesn't start on time, conversation hogs, negative conflicts, rambling discussions or simply an exchange of useless information. We cannot control all participants, but we can certainly control our own contributions as a participant during meetings and try to insist on others starting on time and following an established agenda. When you chair a meeting, keep it crisp and productive. Keep the discussion of important agenda items brief and follow up with a decision, a time frame and an assignment of responsibility. Don't waste time. Even more importantly, think hard about the people who are attending meetings. Do they all need to be there? If the purpose is simply to share information, is there a better way to do so? If the purpose of the meeting is decision making, make sure the right people are in attendance. Avoid inviting others just to be polite. It's a waste of your time and theirs.

Procrastination—I spoke of this already. Handle each piece of paper or each document, report, memo or email once and once only. Read it. Deal with it. Move on. If more information or research is needed, decide what is needed, who can find it and set it aside until all the necessary information is available. Make decisions (more on this in a later chapter). Don't procrastinate.

Water-Cooler Whining—Don't let yourself get drawn into water-cooler whining. This is when people stand around complaining about how terrible things are. It's a waste of time and serves only to bring everyone involved down. Don't be part of it and if you are considered one of the organizational or departmental leaders, make sure it doesn't happen on your watch. If it is happening, determine what or who is at the root of the problem and deal with it. Taking a break during the day and chatting with colleagues about various issues can be positive for all concerned, but if the chats become "whine sessions," they can no longer be considered to be productive.

Multitasking—For the most part, we are usually impressed by the ability to multitask, but it can be carried to the extreme and affect our ability to focus on anything meaningful. Multitasking is fine as long as it is productive and is not used as a regular routine. It is a time-waster if work isn't accomplished in terms of its volume or quality. If we take on too much or fail to focus effectively enough on the job at hand, it may result in mistakes or poor quality. The multitasker must remain focused, but sadly, so many who try to routinely multitask are often the same ones that have so much difficulty focusing on any one thing.

Micromanaging—I was always taught that, as a leader, I should aim to work myself out of a job. Organize the department, assign work to everyone and let them do their job. Far too many managers organize and assign but then feel compelled to micromanage. I have already stated my case against micromanagers. As I said earlier, if it takes two people to do one job, one of those two people isn't necessary. Either you are doing a lousy job or your employee is. Don't waste anyone's time.

At the end of the day, we only have so much time. Unfortunately, so many of us fail to use what limited amount of time we have to its fullest value. Many of us can waste time we have as well as that of others and, if we're doing that, we are extending no respect to the people we deal with. Don't be late and don't be a time-waster. Show respect for others and honour your time commitments.

Principle #6

Communicate, Communicate, Communicate

I went to the doctor because I was concerned that my wife's hearing was getting worse (not really, but bear with me). He told me to do a little test when I got home. So when I got home I went to a point in the house about 50 feet from where she was preparing supper and said, "Honey, what's for dinner?" No answer. So I moved a little closer, about 40 feet away and again said, "Honey, what's for dinner?" Again, no reply. I moved to a point about 30 feet away and said, "Honey, what's for dinner." No answer. I was getting quite concerned as I moved to a point about 20 feet away and repeated the question and again received no answer. Finally I moved to about 10 feet away and said, "Honey, what's for dinner?" And finally, I got an answer—she shouted rather abruptly, "For the fifth time, roast beef!!" Perhaps we had a communication problem and perhaps the fault was not hers.

Over the course of my years in leadership roles, I have discovered that in almost every organization, concerns are occasionally expressed about the amount or quality of communications in the business. It is worse for some than it is for others, but almost invariably, it is never seen to be perfect. In fact, some times, the harder we work to improve communications, the more people seem to complain. If we stop to consider the best messages we have ever heard, we may better understand what makes them effective and how we may be able to improve our own communications.

First, let us consider the words of astronaut John Swigert Jr. when he simply said, "Houston, we have a problem." At the time and under the circumstances, those five words may have caused the hearts of some of the folks in Houston to skip a beat or two. What about Dr. Martin Luther King Jr. when he said, "I have a dream!" Those four words caused a nation to sit up and pay attention. Messages don't necessarily have to be delivered by famous people. When we are kids and we get too close to the stove, our parents say, "Don't touch. It's hot!" The local soccer coach needs to communicate with kids using terms they will understand. The Rotary Club president or the members, when promoting an event, service or fundraiser, need to ensure that the words they use are easily understood by their audience. In each case, the message needs to be kept simple, without the use of jargon and delivered by a trusted source.

I understand that John Swigert Jr. had to go into some technical detail to explain why he had a problem or that some jargon or technical descriptions will be necessary if one needs to describe the inner workings of a nuclear reactor. However, to every extent possible, we need to remember to keep messages short, sweet and uncomplicated. I am a bit of a technological dinosaur and recently came across an effective example of what confusion poor communication can cause. This happened when a person, who is very comfortable in the social media world, sent me an email and suggested that I needed to do something with my website to make it more effective. I say "something" in this case because her message was only two or three sentences long but they were so cluttered with jargon that I had no idea what was being said. As a result, I simply deleted her message since it achieved nothing but cause me frustration.

Several years ago, as vice-president of human resources of a hospital in Ontario, I had the displeasure of handing out a large number of layoff notices. It was part of a downsizing initiative intended to reduce operating costs. My intent was to be open and honest with all staff and I felt a degree of compassion was in order for what would be a very difficult situation for each of them. Therefore, my letter to each one noted that they were to be laid off, when it would happen and what their options were. If they had any questions, they could contact their union representative. Alternatively, my door was always open and they were welcome to discuss things with me and I would do what I could to help (this was the compassion part). In terms of communication, each and every one of them understood my message very clearly. In fact, it was too clear. I think each and every one of them took advantage of my offer to drop in and visit. During their visits they made it abundantly clear to me what a jackass I was and I soon became the lightning rod for all their collective social ills, the cause (in the minds of many) of marriage failures, mortgage foreclosures, wayward children, drug and alcohol problems and every other evil imaginable.

The truth of the matter is that I failed to appreciate that the history of the hospital and its culture had always been like one big, happy family. Layoffs were never part of any operating mantra nor had anyone ever remotely imagined such an eventuality. While it may not have been my decision to make, this was a case where the people wanted to shoot the messenger. As it turned out, I was eventually welcomed back into the "family" and was far more careful about how I communicated from that point forward. I had learned a great lesson about communication. Always consider your audience.

These communications challenges are not in the exclusive purview of the workplace. We see them regularly at the home with our kids, our neighbours, our families and anywhere else we care to consider. How many marriages break up because the partners no longer communicate? How many of us have difficulty communicating with our kids or parents for a variety of reasons resulting in serious frustration? Everything we do in life, at home, at work and in the community involves communications of some kind. So, how do we take the steps necessary to bring about improvements in such a simple process?

Let's start with challenges that come in this age of extensive electronic communications. Does any of this sound familiar? Have you ever:

- Sent a message entirely in CAPS thinking, perhaps, it was easier to read that way only to learn that it is the electronic equivalent of shouting at the recipient?
- Wondered what LOL meant the first time you saw it?

- Had a colleague or lawyer use our completely innocent words against us in an attempt to convey a totally different meaning than what was intended?
- Had a newspaper, radio or TV reporter misquote us or take words out of context that ultimately conveyed the wrong message to the public?
- Had people question you about your voice-mail message and wonder what sort of mood you were in when you recorded it? (I was in a great mood—going on vacation—why do you ask?)
- Faced a circumstance where you have felt that you have gone above and beyond in communicating a message repeatedly, clearly and to every possible person affected by the issue, only to have one or more people casually remark that "communications sure suck around here."
- Unintentionally added a name to a group distribution message or sent a message to an unintended recipient that later caused untold embarrassment.

They have all happened to me and under slightly different circumstances may likely have happened, to some extent, to each of us.

Real estate professionals will often state that the three most important considerations when buying are "location, location, location." For the purposes of this chapter, our three most important words are "communicate, communicate, communicate" (and, when you have done that, communicate some more). But, why is it that so many of us routinely screw it up?

How Does Communication Happen?

If we consider communications as a simple exchange of information among two or more people, then it involves a sender, a receiver and a message via some kind of medium. We could add that there is a feedback loop that allows the receiver to confirm understanding of the message with the sender. Sadly, it has been suggested that we tend to retain only 10 percent of what we hear and 20 percent of what we read. The rest is lost. Like so many other aspects of life, communication is seldom simplistic. And the reality is that the quality of any given exchange may be affected by a host of variables, ranging from the traits of the sender to the medium used to conflicting noise or message to the mood or disposition of either the sender or the receiver. Let's have a look at some of these as they apply to leaders in particular.

Communication Skills of Leaders

If we consider the communication styles of people who many of us consider to be world leaders, both from the past and present, one of the qualities that most often becomes so evident is their oratorical skills. They can hold an audience of one or even millions spellbound by their words. Nelson Mandela, Winston Churchill, John F. Kennedy, Barack Obama, Bill Clinton and Dr. Martin Luther King Jr. all possess or possessed that attribute. However, does the same hold true for our day-to-day organizational and community leaders? Here are nine communication traits and skills that we need to apply consistently if any of us are to be successful as leaders.

1. *Listen very carefully* to what your staff, colleagues, bosses, customers, friends and family are saying. As Stephen R. Covey noted in *The 7 Habits of Highly Effective People*, "seek first to understand, then to be understood."[10] Too often, we try to multitask or anticipate what others are about to say or simply do not focus on the message being delivered. I was always told that the Good Lord gave us two ears and one mouth so we could listen twice as much as we talked. Too many people get these reversed and insist on talking twice as much as listening. Focus on what others are saying to you, and if you listen to people very carefully and confirm complete understanding, all parties will be ultimately better served in the relationship.

2. *Maintain an open door.* While this may not initially appear to be a communications issue, it certainly contributes positively to the appearance of receptivity of some leaders. Philosophically, if you maintain an open door, you also maintain an open mind. If you perpetually stay behind closed doors, the impression is given that you are not open to a free exchange of information, that new ideas

are not welcome and that communication will be difficult at best. The philosophy of one outstanding leader I know was to "have a reason to close your door, not a reason to open it." On occasion, as I noted on managing your time, you may need to close your door but, under most circumstances, you will enjoy more positive and open communication if you just leave your door open.

3. In line with maintaining an open door, is the importance of being *approachable and available.* We all know of people who leave their doors open but, as to being approachable, there is simply no sense of warmth or welcome about them. As a result, the best approach to them is no approach at all. Ultimately, it serves only to stifle communication. Similarly, there are some who are approachable but that's only good if they are available. If they are otherwise occupied outside of the workplace or organization or fail to respond to emails, voice mails or other messages, again, the result is that communication is stifled.

4. It may sound odd in this day and age but we should all promote *face-to-face* communications. Make it comfortable. As noted above, be approachable or, just be nice to people. Your staff, customers, family and neighbours will all be much happier and much more effective in their communications if you deal with them in a more personal fashion. If at all possible, don't send an email to a person seated 20 feet away. If you can, visit that person. Do lunch or breakfast. Invite them to your place for tea and discussion. It will increase the odds of you improving the quality of all your communications.

5. I mentioned it earlier but it is worth mentioning again. Beware of using jargon in your communications. This includes making assumptions that others understand not only the words and expressions you are using but also that we sometimes assume that others may even know what we're thinking when communicating something to them. We have all done it from time to time. And though, after having been happily married for 38 years, I may like to believe that I know what my wife is thinking most of the time or she may believe she knows what I am thinking, it's not always a healthy position to take in our communications. In addition to

keeping it simple and not making assumptions, leaders need to appear confident in their messages without being arrogant. If you lack that confidence, those on the receiving end of your messages may find them lacking in credibility.

6. Remember the *non-verbal* aspects of communications. Watch your body language. What does it tell others about you? Do you cross your arms when speaking with staff? It suggests an unreceptive attitude. Remember to smile. It's infectious. Look people in the eye when you speak with them. How do you dress? What does that convey? Are you working your cell phone when you're supposed to be listening to somebody? It's not just what you say that's important but there are other elements to your communications. One popular television show from a few years back (but still in syndication) takes pokes at close talkers, high talkers, low talkers, loud talkers and mumblers. What does your own style say about you?

7. People prefer to deal with others that they can count on as being *candid or authentic*. Part of being authentic means that what we think is consistent with what we say and both are consistent with what we feel and do. There must be no inconsistencies in our behaviour. This does not necessarily mean that we have to be brutally frank with people (although it sometimes helps), but I would rather deal with someone I can count on for straightforward answers and that means for both good news and bad news. There can be no lies, no exaggerations from leaders. We all need to count on good, sound advice, counsel and support. The importance of candor and authenticity for leaders in their relations with others while at work, at home or in the community can never be overstated.

8. True leaders can be counted on to be consistent in the messages they deliver. Perhaps this is included in the other traits mentioned but I feel it deserves special attention. The manner in which we approach issues, discussions and decisions from one day to the next communicates a great deal about us to others. Consistency in our approach, in our demeanour, in being available and in being calm

under fire will promote confidence and comfort which, in turn, will significantly aid communications for every kind of leader.

9. Let's be honest. We all screw up from time to time. The leader we should all aspire to be, whether at work, at home or in the community, will step up to the plate and acknowledge mistakes. When we are kids and get caught by the teacher for not having completed our homework, the easy escape is always to blame others or tell the teacher that "the dog ate my homework." That doesn't work as adults and for leaders. We do not blame others and, in fact, may occasionally take the blame on behalf of our team. Effective communication includes the ability to say to others, "I screwed up." It is most often followed by something like, "Here's how I plan to make it good."

What About the Message Itself?

In the movie *Cool Hand Luke,* one of the guards, after he has physically abused one of the prisoners, proclaims, "What we have here is a failure to communicate.". Oh, how often is that the case? Communication can be and should be simple. Why is it that we make it complicated and convoluted sometimes? We can all communicate much more effectively if we keep it simple. As I have already noted, we love to use jargon, acronyms and slang. All of these are fine as long as both sender and receiver understand the exact meaning given to the jargon and the context in which it is used. It seems that all professional groups or associations have their own terms and expressions which may be quite meaningless to people outside the profession. Remember your audience and communicate accordingly. Also, remember that your message may be affected by variables such as your mood or the mood of your receiver. It may sound like a recipe card, but keep it simple and repeat as necessary.

There is another aspect of communication that may be something of a double-edged sword and is part of every community and every organization. There is no sense trying to get rid of it. It's not going away. Know that it is there and, in some cases, you can even take advantage of it. I'm speaking of gossip and "the grapevine"!!

Earlier in my career, I had the pleasure of teaching college courses in organizational behaviour. One of the fun activities that we tried each year was to see what happened when a simple message is communicated from one person to another verbally. Try it sometime in a group of 10 to 15 people (larger groups work even better but the exercise is effective enough at this size). The message would be something like the following:

> *Mary Muller and Mike Martin were married in the North Bay United Church on Saturday May 16, 2004 at 2:00 p.m. in front of 200 friends and family members. Following the ceremony, all guests attended a reception at the Green Briar Country Club and enjoyed a beautiful prime rib dinner with all the usual trimmings. The newlyweds honeymooned in Ottawa, Montreal and Vermont. They will be settling in Quebec City where Mary works as a civil engineer and Mike has since joined the Montreal Hospital as a laboratory technologist.*

By the time the last person tells the class what he/she understands to be the original message, it will have changed rather dramatically. Instead of getting married, they were often getting divorced or worse. Most gossip and grapevine information is simply inaccurate. It is not believable and a true leader does not engage in gossip, does not want to hear it in the first place and most assuredly refuses to pass it along. However, most of us do come to terms with it and learn who among us is a key link in the grapevine machinery and which of our colleagues can be trusted to share only legitimate and reliable information. Always be alert to grapevine information, take everything they say with a grain of salt, but remember that it may also serve to give you a sense for the pulse of the organization as well as the concerns, issues and beliefs of staff. As a result, whatever redeeming qualities it has may be limited.

The Message Is in the Medium: How Leaders Communicate

The medium that we use will depend on who we are communicating with, why, what the message is about and the degree of urgency involved. Hopefully, it is obvious by now that I favour face-to-face communication, with individuals or groups, if at all possible. However, should that not be possible, we enjoy a host of other forms of communication, including phone, email, memos, cell phones and the internet. The biggest advantage of face-to-face communication is that there is the opportunity for a full exchange of information, clarification as necessary and, as important as anything, access to non-verbal clues and the message conveyed by body language. Nevertheless, face-to-face communication is not always possible, in which case, everything else is second best.

Remember, anything you put in writing is always subject to interpretation and being misconstrued, so be careful. There have been too many occasions when I have seen feelings hurt or actions taken based on misinformation. All this because of poor sentence structure, improper use of words or phrases or a simple misinterpretation caused by the mood or disposition of the sender while delivering the message or the receiver at the time of receipt. Also, remember that anything you submit in writing can be traced and kept, in perpetuity, to be held against you at a later date and time. Don't ever think that, just because you deleted an email message, the means to find it again do not exist. Good communication skills demand that we are careful about what we say and how we say it. But it is especially critical, for our own personal protection in the future, that we choose our words and phrases ever so shrewdly in any written communication.

In addition to one-on-one communications, there is often a need to convey messages to groups of people. In days gone by, the preferred method was via the company memo or newsletter. Those approaches still exist and are still effective. However, most organizations also have some form of intranet available which allows access to and by most employees. Additional modes available to us include websites, town-hall type meetings and hotlines for various purposes. Finally, let's not forget that every organization has its share of official reports and forms that are all part of the communications network. Memos and reports are expected to adhere to some predetermined format. All forms, budgets, forecasts, performance appraisals, etc., are intended to communicate messages to assorted audiences. Use them effectively.

Finally, if the essence of communication is that it is the exchange of information among two or more people, then truly, the most profound change that has occurred in recent years has been the introduction of social media. Web-based media platforms such as Facebook, Twitter, LinkedIn or YouTube have become immensely popular on both personal and business fronts. Though the quality of messages sent and received via social media can never match face-to-face interactions, there can be no denying that the reach, frequency and immediacy of these media far exceed anything that the more traditional media sources can ever achieve. We have all seen examples of newsworthy items (and some not so newsworthy) that have gone viral and reached millions of readers in a matter of hours. No email, memo or newspaper could ever hope to achieve such widespread and virtually instantaneous coverage. The amount of time being spent on social media sites around the world is increasing at a phenomenal rate as more and more individuals not only join various sites but also check in on them throughout the day.

Social media can be a wonderful tool and opportunity for any leader for several reasons. First, as noted, the reach enjoyed and the opportunity to contact so many in such short periods of time, at such low cost cannot be matched by any other means available. However, one must be careful not to sacrifice quality of contacts or "friends" for the sake of having large numbers. Second, in addition to simple communications, social media opens up incredible marketing opportunities for companies as they seek to promote themselves or their products. Again, acquiring quality contacts, who are more likely to take advantage of those products or services, is more valuable than simply getting as many contacts as possible. Third, social media offers an opportunity to connect effectively and engage in virtual conversations with customers and others. A newsletter, advertisement or press release tends to be one way only and stops once the message has been delivered while social media allows an exchange of information or ideas; it becomes two-way. We can be sincere. We can be real without worrying quite so much about being absolutely, politically correct. Fourth, use of social media allows us to monitor what is happening in our industry, get feedback from customers, and find out about emerging trends or things to be aware of or opportunities to take advantage of. Clearly, it is a means of (as I discuss in a later chapter) scanning the horizon and that is something all leaders need to do.

Notwithstanding the wonderful opportunities that come with the use of social media, I would hasten to add a couple of cautions. Like most of the information we find on the internet, there is no guarantee of its accuracy or trustworthiness. Not everyone who uses social media or posts blogs is 100 percent scrupulous or believable. This serves as another reason to focus on quality contacts rather than quantity. In addition, as many people have unfortunately discovered, it is wise to not post anything on Facebook, Twitter or other sites that you don't want the entire world to know about. For example, staff have often been fired based on postings that generated negative publicity for their employer. How many young people (and perhaps some older ones too) have not yet figured out that posting naked pictures of themselves or other unflattering images or information has a nasty habit of going unintentionally viral? Remember, any such information should be considered to be permanent and may easily come back to haunt you even 10 years from now. Be proper. Be polite. Be professional.

Social media is a great way for leaders to communicate effectively with others. However, it is only a tool, and like all tools must be used properly and with the best of intentions in mind. In addition, as with all tools, it must be properly maintained. Having a page that is not maintained or is out-of-date is not only unhelpful but in fact, may be damaging to your reputation.

Communications during Change Initiatives

Various experts have suggested that between 80 percent and 90 percent of all change initiatives fail due to communications problems. Leaders keep an eye on the horizon and as such, they both anticipate and, as necessary, make changes. But changes bring biases with them. For some, there is comfort with the status quo. For others, change is seen as unnecessary or even a movement in the wrong direction. Regardless, change agents must be prepared to be challenged and, while they may see the advantages of the new way and the disadvantages of the old, others will not be so convinced. It is at these times that we must be prepared to *communicate, communicate, communicate*. Depending on the extent of the changes envisioned, messages may take every form, ranging from face-to-face meetings to focus group sessions (for both input and feedback) to newsletters, intranet messages, social media postings and everything in between.

It is also important to be aware of who the unofficial organization leaders are. They may be union leaders, the social butterflies or just the grapevine masters. Every organization and every community has one such group. While you may resent such groups and their influence, as a leader you would be wise to utilize them to every extent possible.

During change initiatives, the messages must be multidirectional and should match the perspectives of the intended audiences. There can be no such thing as too much information but there can be mixed messages, so beware of having too many people sending official communications, especially during times of major changes. Only one person should be responsible and a consistent message should be conveyed. If you fail to be transparent during change initiatives and fail to communicate regularly and effectively, you risk having people challenge the change. They may make false assumptions, fuel the rumour mill, become angry and frustrated with your leadership or, ultimately, disrupt the entire initiative. Be prepared. You can almost be certain that challenges will be forthcoming.

Principle #7

A Customer Focus

There is a story that is told of a situation in a hospital's intensive care unit. It was noticed that patients always died in the same bed, on a Sunday morning, at about 11:00 a.m., regardless of their medical condition. This puzzled the doctors and some even thought it had to do with the supernatural. Nobody could solve the mystery as to why the deaths occurred around 11:00 a.m. Sunday. A worldwide team of experts was assembled to investigate the cause of the incidents. The next Sunday morning, a few minutes before 11:00 a.m. all of the doctors and nurses nervously waited outside the ward to see for themselves what the terrible phenomenon was all about. Some were holding wooden crosses, prayer books and other holy objects in order to ward off the evil spirits. Just as the clock struck 11:00, Jimmy Johnson, the part-time Sunday cleaner, entered the ward and unplugged the life support system so he could plug in his vacuum cleaner. Oops! Customer service or not?

In their book *In Search of Excellence*, Tom Peters and Robert Waterman write that placing customers at the forefront of every business decision is not only critical for the very survival of the business but it also makes good common sense.[11] How can we possibly be successful or cater to our customers' needs if we have no idea of what their needs or wants are? We need to focus on our customers because, in the final analysis, they represent our very reason for being. Also, regardless of the type of leader you are, there will always be a customer. It may be a client that a lawyer serves, a retail customer, a taxpayer, your own family or community. While a stay-at-home parent may think of his/her charges as "just the kids," in essence they remain customers that need the services provided by the parent. That is why the parent chooses to stay at home.

Similarly, Weiss and Molinaro claim that there are five ways that leaders can demonstrate a strong customer focus:

- They hear the customer's voice in everything they do. Obviously, this is not meant to be a literal matter but rather, when products or services are considered, decisions are made or plans set in motion, they must first consider how the customer will react or respond to those actions.
- They must be advocates for their customers. This is part of building a relationship with them. If you sell a product or service and offer nothing further in the relationship, the customers will soon seek out another supplier. As an added value, your business should lead by promoting and advocating on behalf of the customer. If you can't do that for legal or ethical reasons, you need to reconsider whether or not you should keep them as a client.
- They make changes that are only customer driven. True leaders know how to respond to change, adapt to it and, in fact, act proactively in promoting it, but they do not change purely for the sake of change. Product or service changes that are of no value to the customer may increase the risk that the customer may soon be lost.
- They know and understand the customers' value chain. Everything and everybody connected with the customer has a value that a true leader is aware of and recognizes the importance of.
- They articulate a clear connection between their own organizational and personal objectives and values and those of their customers.[12]

Even when a successful organization such as Southwest Airlines claims to place their customers as second best, second only to their own staff, the real purpose in keeping staff happy is that customers will be the ultimate benefactors of a happy staff. In *NUTS!* authors by Kevin and Jackie Freiberg make the following claim:

> Southwest wants its customers to experience service that makes a
> lasting impression, service that is kind and loving, service that is
> fun and makes them laugh. The company believes that treating
> people with respect and dignity is the key to providing its unique
> brand of Positively Outrageous Service. Thus, Southwest will
> go a long way to defend and support an employee who may
> violate a company policy to bend toward the customer. The
> company instills in every employee the idea that happy, satisfied
> customers who return again and again create job security.[13]

If customers see disgruntled employees, they soon seek to take their
business elsewhere. We all want to deal with staff that are happy, content
and likeable.

In addition to what Tom Peters and Robert Waterman, David Weiss and
Vince Molinaro, and Kevin and Jackie Freiberg have said about customer
relations, one of the operating philosophies that I regularly promote is
called servant leadership. I suppose there are those who consider it a
model of leadership but my approach is that servant leadership really
delivers a way or an approach to how we conduct ourselves as leaders. We
should do everything in our power to inspire those we lead to do better.
As they become inspired, they deliver better performances and as their
performances improve, the ultimate benefactor is the customer, client or
taxpayer.

No matter how we slice it, regardless of the nature of our leadership, there
is always a customer, which is ultimately the reason for our being, the
reason for our product or service and a good reason to get out of bed in
the morning. For each and every one of us, there is a customer that needs
to be satisfied. The questions that must be answered by each of us include:
Who are our customers? How do we satisfy them and how do we hear
their voice in every decision we make? What are they telling us? How do
they affect our strategic plans? These are just some of the questions that
we need to consider. There will always be others but let's start by getting a
grasp on who our customers are.

Who Are My Customers?

In some instances, it may be relatively easy to identify our customers. A car dealership sells or leases vehicles to members of the public: individuals, organizations, fleet, and so on. It doesn't really matter. The customer is obvious. This applies to all those who are engaged in direct sales to the public, regardless of the exact nature of the products, whether they be cars, hamburgers, furniture, shoes or houses. When you sell a product to the public it is relatively easy to determine who your customers are. Similarly, industrial sales, services providers and consultants should have readily identifiable customers. Other leaders don't have it so easy. When customers are organizations, do they always know their customers' customers? Service departments may find customer definition to be trickier. Support service departments such as finance, human resources, information technology, legal, purchasing, receiving, all have similar challenges. What about teachers? Are their customers the student? The parent? The taxpayer? Perhaps all of the above? What about the hockey or soccer coaches? Who do they consider to be their customers? Even the stay-at-home parent has customers. While their families may not pay them as such for services rendered, parents still deliver a service and, therefore, I would suggest that the kids, spouses and others be considered as their customers. The answers to these questions, as far as this book is concerned, are immaterial. The thinking that goes into answering them is far more important. Regardless of who your customers are, outstanding leaders will reach out to them, truly understand their needs and respond accordingly.

What Is the Nature of Our Customers?

About five years ago, I was told that I was the proud possessor of a "Morton's Neuroma," which sounds awful but really doesn't amount to much more than a little thing on my foot. Just prior to receiving that news, I had been advised that I needed three dental implants. If I had been told the same things 20 years ago I would have simply trusted the medical practitioners that shared the good news with me and said, "Okay, let's do it.". But that was then, and this is now. It's not that I didn't trust the practitioners but, like so many others in today's world, after speaking with each one, I decided to seek out one more opinion and referred to everyone's favourite source of infinite wisdom, the internet.

I pointed out earlier that you should approach information found on the internet with some skepticism. However, there are times when it serves a purpose in helping to educate us in specific situation. It helped me in both situations that I faced and it helps many of us in a host of other ways. I suspect that we all take a similar approach when facing medical challenges or even just when buying a new home, a new car, TV or just need information on a product or service. The reality today is that our customers are not as gullible or perhaps they have access to so much more information than they once did. This means that our customers are much more knowledgeable about our products, our services and our competition than ever before. However, let me remind you that there are limited controls on the information that is so readily available, so everything we read must be taken with a grain of salt. Be prepared to correct any misinformation your customers might bring to you.

This leads me to what Peter S. Pande has referred to as the "Law of the Ignorant Customer." In an ideal world, a customer's search for valid, reliable information should lead, in turn, to a frank discussion of the product or service, its strengths and weaknesses and its status relative to the competition. However, this is not an ideal world and customers may occasionally be misled or otherwise inclined to make unwise decisions. The emphasis of Pande's Law is that customers sometimes don't even know what they want or what they should expect from the suppliers of products or services. Pande points out six important facts to remember about customers:

1. Customers have other personal or organizational priorities that may lead them to place less emphasis on their dealings with you than they should. A supplier may have a superior product for me but if my brother-in-law sells something similar, albeit inferior, I may, for the sake of family relations, buy from my brother-in-law.
2. They are not expert in your products or services so don't expect them to be. Part of the job of a sales person is to, with integrity, convince a customer of the merits of their product.

3. They have their own organizational silos, politics and bureaucracies which may occasionally impair sound decision making.

4. They often spend more time fighting fires then they do preventing them. As a result, their priorities change with each day and each crisis. They often don't take time to think things through and make sound decisions.

5. Remember, especially for organizations that are buying a product used to be sold elsewhere, if they often don't understand their own customers' needs, the entire supply chain may be adversely affected.

6. In many cases, customers may they *think* they know about the product or their needs but that "knowledge" is, in fact, wrong or at least their reasoning about it may be faulty.[14]

None of this means that we can't be customer focused. However, remember that the customer, contrary to old adage, may not always be right. For the moment, recognizing that our customers are not always infinitely wise for the reasons described above, will help us to respond more effectively to their needs and wants. As such, it is important that we know our customers and the nature of their business and that we anticipate, as much as possible, their issues and challenges. However, before even beginning to understand those customers, it is important that we have an appreciation of the kind of customer we would like to attract.

Each of us should have an image or impression of the type of customer we would like to deal with. Presumably, while one having deep pockets helps, we look for other features such as those we can trust, who conduct their affairs ethically and legally or those that are interested in making the world a better place. Perhaps, it may be someone who holds values that are similar to our own, treats their family and staff well or regularly gives back to their community. It may be simply somebody we like. Leaders have high standards for themselves and others. Don't waiver from your own standards.

Relationship Building

There are two parties involved in the building and maintenance of any relationship—you and the other person. It's really quite simple. However, for the purposes of this discussion, the parties are the leader and the customer. Because I am promoting the notion that true leaders are customer focused, the leader should be trying diligently to fully understand and be concerned about everything that the customer is. This starts with simply knowing who your customer is as well as his/her essential nature. Organizationally, the relationship starts as we construct our mission, vision, values and every measure we use to determine our success or lack thereof.

In the case of Walt Disney World, one of the cornerstones of its operations is that there must be Four Guest Expectations:

- Make me feel special
- Treat me as an individual
- Respect me and my children
- Be knowledgeable

Every staff member at Disney is taught to fulfill these expectations at every given opportunity.

Disney enjoys an outstanding reputation for customer service and that is perhaps something every organization and every individual should aspire to achieve. However, for many of the small enterprises in the world or even for community-based organizations, parents, unions or coaches, the reality is that we all need our customers, we want them all to be happy with us and we want them to be satisfied with our services. Even for something as routine as the HR department at the Region of Durham where I was last employed as Commissioner of HR, we had a mission statement that focused on our customers. It read as follows:

> *We are each committed to partnering with our customers, to provide excellence in service and to deliver effective Human Resources initiatives and programs which contribute to the achievement of organizational goals.*

We tried to ensure that our values lined up with the region's corporate strategic plan by dedicating ourselves to the fulfillment of those values that included the delivery of excellent service to our taxpayers—our customers. Our measures, taken every year via a simple survey, used four key performance indicators: response time, accessibility, quality of service and professionalism. Once again, the measures reflected our service to our customers. Frankly, we were hardly unique in this regard. These mission statements, values and measures were not the only ones that could be considered. Most contemporary departments, services and organizations attempt to reflect a relationship with their customers, and the starting point is their mission statement, vision, values and measures. What separates good leaders and organizations from the mediocre ones is putting the words into actions.

For most of us, putting our intentions into action is a significant challenge. There are four key things we can do to achieve this.

The first thing to do is to follow The Golden Rule and build relationships on a foundation of mutual respect. I noted earlier the importance of this rule in our role as leaders: Do unto others as you would have them do unto you. In this case, the customer is the other, and, as leaders and staff, we need to put ourselves in the place of our customers. How would we like to be treated? What sort of communications would we enjoy and appreciate? What level of service can we expect? We need to be aware of how our customers define our performance and then we can best achieve that level by determining what is important to them and taking steps to address it.

I further assume that each of us would always expect to be treated with respect and courtesy. That is how we need to treat our customers. We need to constantly hone our listening skills, paying attention to what the customers are saying and responding appropriately. They should trust us and appreciate our honesty and integrity, ultimately believing that we will, at the very least, not do any intentional harm to them. It may sound a little over-the-top but that is how we want them to feel about our product, our service, our organization and about us. The way we can most effectively achieve that level of respect is by maintaining regular, personal contact with them. Voice mail, email and telephone may be well and fine but they will never supplant personal contact. Use it to your full advantage.

The second thing is that to every extent possible, you make yourself indispensable. Whether you sell a product, provide outstanding service, provide delivery arrangements—be so good that your customer cannot function without you and they come to consider you as part of the solution for any operational challenge they may face. You need to become a part of their business, so understand it well. You don't want you customers to explore the option of conducting their business in the future without you. Go above and beyond if your business is service oriented. What more can you do for your customer? How can you help them to sell their product? Can you help them identify operational efficiencies (without being a burden or imposition on them)? These approaches are important regardless of the nature of your business, be it auto parts, home health care, shoe sales or human resources. Always ask the question, "What more can I do to help my customer?" Your customers should come to rely on you as a deliverer of service and someone who is there to help as needed. As noted previously, know what they value, be responsive and show them just how important they are to you.

The third thing requires that a leader always see and consider the big picture. Our HR department supported a number of operating departments. It was my responsibility to see beyond the transactional activities that we are so often engaged in and consider what we may have been able to do to deliver better services to our customers. More will be said about this visioning later. Suffice it to say for now, great leaders always see not only the big picture for themselves but also for their customers.

The fourth thing is that relationship building should address what we want our legacy to be. This becomes especially true for those involved in personal leadership roles like parents or coaches. When we are finished our parenting there is no greater reward than seeing that our children have become fine, upstanding, responsible adults. As their leader, we can take much of the credit for that development. Coaches who help their charges develop their skills on the field or on the ice as well as contribute meaningfully to their development as people play important roles as leaders. Don't ever let the importance of these roles escape you.

So far, everything seems to be pointing toward the importance of the customer and by no means do I wish to suggest anything but that. However, there is the old adage about the customer always being right. Not necessarily true. Balance must always be sought when considering the needs and wants of your customers. In terms of product, if one customer demands a customization that is not wanted by any other customers or makes the product no longer profitable, then we must say NO. If a demand for a service takes you beyond your level of expertise or beyond your comfort zone, again, the answer must be NO. It may be qualified by reference to another service supplier or additional support but trying to do what you know is beyond your limits would only be an injustice to your customer. An HR department must balance the needs of often competing interests of various customers—staff, management, unions, shareholders, taxpayers, and so on. Will all of your customers be happy when you tell them you can't comply with their demands? No, of course not. However, for the sake of your own personal integrity and that of your company, product or service, you must occasionally say NO. Remember, you can please some of the people all of the time and all of the people some of the time but you will never please all of the people all of the time. Think of the big picture and always hear the voice of the customer in every action you take and decision you make. You don't always have to cater to the voice. Just make sure you hear it.

Other aspects of the relationship are just as critical to us as leaders. Some of those include the following:

1. Quite frankly, I want my customers to like me. I hear it mentioned occasionally by some that "I would rather be respected than liked." What a bunch of bunk that is!! If a customer has two potential suppliers of services or products that are equal in all respects but the customer personally likes one supplier and not the other, which one is likely to get the business? You can be both liked and respected. Try to achieve both.

2. You can only ever be responsible for your own behaviour. Make sure it is always beyond reproach. What others do is not as much a concern for you and, if the customer is looking for special deals,

shortcuts or other actions that may be unethical or illegal, you are better served to not have them as a customer. What they do in terms of their behaviour is their business. What you do is yours. That is all that you can control.

3. I want to be able to trust my customers or clients but, more importantly, I want them to trust me. This is the foundation of a truly great customer relationship. Never lose sight of it.

4. Do the little things well for your customers. Remember their names and know them as individuals, not simply customers. If they are having health problems, call to ask how they are. Send them cards to acknowledge them at special times of the year, whatever that may be. Commit to being on time with them. Always look and act professionally. Follow up their questions and concerns immediately. Some of these things only take a moment or two but are of critical importance.

5. Do anything else you can to build and promote a positive relationship, not just by yourself but also by involving staff, your family or others who may represent you with customers or in the community.

What About the Public Sector?

The last piece of the puzzle under the umbrella of customer service relates to differences found in the public sector. For those who work in the public sector, there is less in the way of direct sales to customers of products or services and more in the delivery of services solely intended for the benefit of the public and the taxpayer. (For the record, I recognize that not everyone uses every service equally and we all pay, in part, for things like water usage, recreational programs or pet licensing, but the services I am considering here are those delivered to the taxpayers generally.) This results in the potential for everyone, to be a customer for any level of government service.

Those working in the public sector tend to do so under a perpetual microscope and are subject to more intense scrutiny than most of those working in the private sector. We've all heard the common rallying cry of many a disgruntled taxpayer venting frustration at a public servant: "I pay your salary, ya know!!" This statement suggests that public servants are to provide each and every taxpayer with undivided, loyal and dedicated personal service. While I hope it is obvious that every taxpayer does not reflect this sort of attitude, it is fair to say that taxpayers are demanding to be involved in key community decisions and are becoming involved in earlier stages of various processes. Consider the number of public forums and town hall meetings that are deemed necessary and desirable and have become a key part of significant government decisions. Every municipal meeting (with some very limited exceptions) in most jurisdictions must be published in advance and be open to the public. Most major legislative changes come following the usual but necessary "dog and pony shows" held across the province, state or the country. People expect to be informed and expect to have their say. There are times when issues of critical importance are being considered and hundreds of delegations demand to be heard. These issues may include the location of a new industry, landfill sites, incinerators, group homes, clinics and so on. While many of these may be considered to be good for the community at large, they are almost invariably met with protests from taxpayers. It's okay for the community but not in my backyard is often the prevailing sentiment. This struggle is intensified in many larger centres where an increasingly diversified population demands increasingly diverse solutions to issues.

All of this makes public service extremely challenging but also brings with it the potential for public servants, politicians and community leaders to truly make a difference in their communities. Municipal councillors in most jurisdictions now enjoy a four-year window in which they hope to make their mark. During the pre-election campaigns, they declare their issues and pet projects. In most instances, they have established a name and reputation for themselves and enjoy a certain standing in the community. Once elected, they have a chance to make a difference and will do everything in their power to make their customers happy. If they fail to do so, they may not be re-elected. It becomes a bit more complicated for provincial, state and federal politicians who not only have the issues and pet projects they face in their home communities but also need to consider the bigger picture for the province, state or the country. In fact, their own party politics sometimes cause conflict for them as they may have one view on an issue which represents their constituents but their party takes an opposing view on the matter.

In this environment, staff are guilty of (or at least perceived to be guilty of) becoming complacent in their role, having a CYA (cover your ass) mentality and generally lacking an enthusiasm for customer service. Solutions to problems are often along the lines of "How have we always done it?" or "What can we get away with that will be most cost effective and least disruptive?" Creative problem solving is often left behind in a union environment (most public sector and broader public sector employers are heavily unionized) that sadly fails to recognize and promote individualism or staff who try new ideas, new approaches or demonstrate initiative. Similarly, in many organizations, we fail to pay for performance. Once again, the result is that we all speak of the importance of our customers and serving the public, but going above and beyond is too often limited to a select few individuals.

Regardless of these public sector impediments, it is worth repeating that we must always hear the customers' voices in everything we do. Failure to do so means we have failed in our duty to ourselves, our organizations and, most important, to our customers and taxpayers.

Principle #8

Support One Another

It has been told that a certain private school in Brisbane was faced with a unique problem. A number of 12-year-old girls were beginning to use lipstick and would put it on in the bathroom. That was fine but after they put it on they would press their lips to the mirror leaving dozens of little lip prints. Every night the janitor would remove them and the next day, the girls would put them back. Finally, the janitor and the principle decided what needed to be done to put an end to the ritual. The principle called all the girls to the bathroom and met them there with the janitor. She explained that all these little lip prints were causing a major problem for the janitor who had to clean them off every night. The little princesses were unmoved, so to demonstrate what it meant for the janitor, the principle asked him to show the girls how much effort was required. At that point, he dipped his long-handled squeegee into the toilet and cleaned the mirror with it. There hasn't been a lip print ever since. Team work saved the day.

What do The Three Musketeers, Wayne Gretzky and Jari Kurri, and the Toronto Symphony Orchestra all have in common? The operating credo for The Three Musketeers was "All for one and one for all." They fought together for an entire kingdom and for one common cause. Gretzky and Kurri played together for the Edmonton Oilers and won four consecutive Stanley Cups. The two of them had an uncanny ability to almost know where the other was at all times, racking up 1543 points together over 5 seasons. In addition, I recently attended a performance by the Toronto Symphony Orchestra. To listen to the individual members tuning up before the evening's performance almost brought tears to my eyes (and not tears of joy). What a racket!! I had to question the likelihood of any harmonic convergence occurring in the hours to follow. However, once they began, the sounds that emanated from their collective instruments were beautiful and absolutely synchronized with one another. The secret in each case is that they support each other. They function as a team.

Whenever I start a new position, there are two rules that I lay on my staff on the very first day of the new job. First, they must respect time, theirs and that of everyone else. Second, my expectation is that the entire group will function as a team. We go forward together, as a single unit. Disagreements or differences of opinion are dealt with behind closed doors. I will never tolerate members of the team badmouthing other members of the team out in the organization or, generally, out in public. Up to this point in time, both rules have been clearly understood and respected. So, why is it that I find the notion of "team" to be so critical? Why do we care if we support one another? What exactly is the leader's role in ensuring that the team survives and thrives? Can't we just go out and each do our own job?

The Nature of a Team

In terms of my own definition, I would consider a "team" to be any group of people who come together to achieve a common purpose, one that is more effectively accomplished by their collective and coordinated efforts as opposed to anything done individually. This is especially true when the tasks to be accomplished are of a more complex type. To that end, every member of every team has a role to play. They know their role and how it fits in with every other member's role. They know how to behave, how to resolve conflicts and how to lean on one another and support one another. There is value and comfort in the knowledge that we can achieve far more when we combine the talents, wider skill sets and wisdom of all members of the team. We are able to address more complex situations and potentially generate more innovative solutions. But, we must get past the talking about that team and appreciate the value of the "team" so that we can use the many and varied skill sets of the team members to full advantage.

I have seen my share of departments and organizations that speak of the importance of the team but that function as a group of individuals. We've all heard these old adages: that "Two heads are better than one" or "There is no I in T.E.A.M" or "Many hands make light work" or "One for all and all for one!" Team work applies not only to the workplace but also to the family setting and to community organizations. We don't wish to waste the power found in the concept of the team but before we can truly harness that power, it helps to better understand what types of teams there are, the nature of membership, the value of a team and its members, team members' roles (especially that of the leader) and what it takes to make the whole thing function. Let's first consider some types of teams.

Types of Teams

In our personal lives, we need to be aware of the family as a type of team. In addition, there are various community teams and workplace teams. These teams include traditional, cross functional, self-directed, communities of interest and informal teams.

Family

It may seem a little silly to consider our family as a team but there really is no difference between what we find here and those teams at the workplace or in sports. Each member of the family has a role to play and, to be successful, the family team needs a leader, a role which usually falls to the parents. I appreciate that the traditional family as I am describing it may be disappearing. Regardless, the same principles apply whether there is a mother and father with three kids, a nice home in the suburbs with a white picket fence or a single mom struggling to survive in a small downtown apartment with two kids. In each case, each person in the unit has a role to play. Someone has to ensure that income is coming in and that bills are being paid. Someone needs to teach the kids about life lessons, connect with the school, arrange medical appointments, and so on. It may be one parent and it may be two or, if the extended family is in the picture, there may be aunts, uncles and others who help to make the world go round. The kids also have their own roles to play as helpers, babysitters, and so on. If the family functions as a team, the results will be better for everyone. When all members pull together for the common good of the family, amazing things can happen.

Community

In this group I am including members of the community that come together to make something happen for the good of the community at large. It may include the Rotary, Kinsmen, Kiwanis or other service clubs or it may be the church or hospital auxiliary. There are neighbourhood park associations in many municipalities that promote improved neighbourhood activities for all. There may be hundreds of other groups that exist for the benefit of the community. In each case, success will not fall to one person but will be contingent on the efforts of many and the assorted roles that the many play. Acting as a team is always in everyone's collective best interest.

Traditional

In any organization or workplace of any size, functions are compartmentalized into operating functions and support services. Each of these functions (or departments) has a leader who may be called the manager, supervisor or director. All team members report to some person in the organization, are relatively constant, work in a common location, have clear roles to perform and are given and follow the direction of their leader. As the organization becomes larger and more diverse and as technology and contemporary organizational approaches allow it, there is the possibility that traditional teams become a little less traditional, often taking on characteristics of something more "virtual" as staff work offsite or from their homes. It becomes somewhat more challenging but remains, for the most part, a traditional team.

Cross Functional

Like the traditional team, a cross-functional team has one designated leader but team members come from varied departments. As an example, an organization may be planning to build new headquarters or to move to a new site. One way to make the transition easier is to form teams with members from all departments to address complex construction issues and to coordinate the move from many locations. Organizational mergers, in some industries especially, are a fact of work life. When mergers occur, representatives from all of the merged organizations may need to come together to plan for the new entity. It doesn't have to be done that way, but the odds of success increase when using a team such as this. The important thing is that cross functional teams can be created purely for the purpose of addressing major projects and one-time initiatives.

Self-Directed

These teams can be considered to be leaderless but are not rudderless. They seem to work best in an environment where the members know their jobs well and have a focused task that needs to be addressed. Examples may be the teams that come together to update fire and safety procedures or to conduct job evaluations as part of an organization's compensation system. In each case, a facilitator may be responsible for coordinating activities but has no absolute authority. Rather, members all have expertise in fields or positions that allow them to come together to function effectively without the need for a leader to officially direct their efforts.

Communities of Interest

These are teams that are not part of the official organizational structure but can be of critical importance. They usually come together for some common goal or interest. While they are not part of the official organizational structure, they occasionally benefit from executive support or sponsorship. An example of this would be a staff celebration committee or Christmas Dance Committee. Another example in a slightly different vein would be unions who have no connection to the organizational structure but are certainly important to their members and certainly have significant impact on the ongoing operations of the organization.

Informal

I spoke previously about the power of the grapevine in communications. The grapevine has no status as an official mode of communication but we are all aware of it and, if wise, use it appropriately. Informal teams are much the same. They exist, and, as a leader, if you can determine who belongs, who serves as their informal leader and what they collectively believe in, they can be of immense value. Sometimes, it may be just two or three colleagues who have worked together since the beginning of time. It may be the four or five members of the maintenance staff who are also members of the local bowling league. A number of staff in organizations that I have worked with belong to the Toastmasters Club. Others have formed a golf league. They will always exist. Use them where it is reasonable to do so to full advantage.

Who Are The Members of the Team and Where Do Their Loyalties Lie?

The answer to this question is that it depends! In some cases, the team members may appear obvious. When I was responsible for the HR department, I expected it to function as a team. In this example, the team members are clearly the staff of the department. However, there are sub-teams within the department that are identified by virtue of their division within HR or perhaps because of their association with the client groups to which they have been assigned. On the broader scale of things, all staff found in an organization should be expected to perform as part of the larger organizational team, whether that be 100 staff or 4,000 staff. How can they be effective as members of more than one team? Where do their loyalties lie in the event of a conflict? There is always that potential as we are all members of several different teams at any one point in time and, where conflicts arise, the needs and demands of the lower organizational team must always accede to those of the higher team.

In most organizations of any significant size, a challenge is almost invariably faced as staff who are members of departmental teams are expected to be loyal members of the larger organizational team. They must balance what sometimes appear to be competing and conflicting demands and priorities. If the HR departmental staff are asked to sacrifice one of their own (a layoff) in order to prevent the layoff of another front-line staff member, is their allegiance to the HR team or to the larger organizational team? These sorts of conflicts may be further confounded by any staff member not only belonging to their organizational teams but also, in the case of unionized employees, to their union as well as participating in informal teams.

Leaders must know and understand that these potential conflicts exist and do what they can to balance the competing interests that their staff may face. There is no easy answer. In fact, these sorts of conflicts also appear in the home where loyalties may be divided between responsibilities at home versus roles to be played at work or in other community groups. An easy example would be when my wife needs to go out to an association meeting and needs me to be home to watch the kids. I might say that I have a board meeting to attend and so the games begin. When those games do begin, the leaders will always stand tall to do the right thing.

Team Values and Identity

For a team to be effective all members must share a sense of purpose and an understanding of why the team exists and what its ultimate goals are. In my last senior HR position, I asked one of the staff to lead the others in a discussion regarding what we collectively saw as the attributes of an HR professional. The results became the values which we collectively agreed to abide by. The following represents the essence of the six core values we agreed to as well as the behaviours found within each of those core values that we collectively came to expect of ourselves:

1. A focus on internal/external customer relationships.
    *   We solve problems and work collaboratively
    *   We are positive, courteous, helpful and respectful
    *   We give customers our undivided attention
    *   We investigate and follow up on customer inquiries and/or concerns
    *   We deal with customers in a timely and efficient manner

- We practice 100 percent service excellence during all customer encounters
- We actively network among regional colleagues and external contacts

2. An interest in working as a team.
    - We actively participate in meetings and group activities
    - We collaborate with others to problem solve, to stimulate innovation and change
    - We strive to achieve a common goal
    - We willingly share pertinent information with others
    - We are tactful and treat others with respect

3. Demonstrate integrity.
    - We demonstrate: honesty, trustworthiness, dependability, professionalism, accountability and responsibility
    - We can be trusted to keep promises and commitments
    - We respect and maintain confidentiality

4. Maintain high quality standards/desire for continuous improvement.
    - We always strive to do better
    - We are always open to change
    - We demonstrate innovation wherever possible
    - We are effective and efficient
    - We act upon customer feedback and lessons learned
    - We are positive possibility thinkers

5. Promotion of excellence in interpersonal/ communication skills.
    - We promote open two-way communications
    - We actively listen and ask questions
    - We are pleasant and polite
    - We treat others with respect
    - We resolve conflicts proactively

- We express ideas/opinions in a positive, assertive manner
- We are open to other points of view
- We are considerate of diversity issues

6. Demonstrate excellence in HR services and technical expertise.
   - We know our products/services and believe in them
   - We commit to our own continuous learning and development
   - We are aware of upcoming HR trends/issues
   - We are cognizant of our businesses and structures

I know these values are lengthy, but what is more important is that I didn't dictate what values the staff, my team, would believe in. They established this for themselves and I merely supported it. Once completed, we had the document laminated and posted throughout the department. While this may not be perfect for every team, it certainly seemed to work for us. There may be other and better approaches that different systems, departments and organizations could apply to meet their own needs.

I also asked the team to consider a lengthy list of traits and skills of effective leaders and advise me of their expectations of me as their department leader. Like the attributes exercise discussed above, this was conducted without me being present. I felt that it was important for them to feel unconstrained by my presence (not that I am particularly intimidating) but to know that I would support whatever they decided to spell out. We created the team values and they followed up by telling me what their expectations of me were. Those expectations were:

- Empower others
- Foster open two-way communication
- Demonstrate and promote integrity
- Be respectful
- Think strategically
- Encourage continuous learning

Again, this document was laminated and, to my very last day with that organization, it was posted on my bulletin board. Both documents served as perpetual guiding lights for me and the members of my team. Notwithstanding their importance to the department, these values should never be seen as carved in stone. To that end, my advice to anyone who cares to listen would be to occasionally take time to review and update values and expectations by using this type of exercise.

Not all teams spell things out so clearly but to be effective the members must share some common values, know who they are and what they stand for. I also made it clear, as part of my rule about team spirit, that it is intolerable for members to gossip about one another unless, of course, the intent is to brag about and extol the virtues of other members to the public at large. Spreading negative gossip or that which is intended to be injurious to other members is inexcusable.

Team Members' Roles

For traditional or departmental type teams, the roles are usually obvious. In larger organizations there is an expectation conveyed by a higher authority that a department has been created in order to accomplish an established goal. Each year, at budget time, the goals are reiterated, refined, expanded and aligned with other organizational services and supported by approved fiscal resources. However, not all teams have such clearly established tasks, although, in order to be successful, it's really not a bad idea. In the case of cross-functional teams or those with a simple community of interest or even self-directed teams, tasks may be very broadly defined initially but need to be more precisely spelled out before the team can move ahead. In addition to spelling out the tasks for the team, there must also be a means of measuring success (or lack thereof) and in communicating those results with the group at large. This becomes the leader's role. He/she must work with their team to ensure that all players not only know what the overall goal for the team is but also how that goal fits into the bigger picture and how success in achieving it will be measured. Part of that process includes identifying priorities (in the case of multiple goals) and determining individual tasks and roles as part of the team. What are those priorities and roles?

Team Priorities and Members' Roles

For many teams, the goals are not as simple as declaring that "we will win the Stanley Cup." A business unit will have production goals, efficiency goals, staff related goals, and so on, all of which must be identified and prioritized. In addition, members must know their individual roles and their assigned tasks as well as knowing how they fit into the larger departmental and organizational priorities. The leader's role in this regard is to determine the respective goals and priorities, organize individuals such that their roles mesh to form a dynamic, effective whole—a kind of well-oiled machine. In this way, the leader's role is no different than that of a leader of a professional sports team or even the local girls' soccer team. In order to be successful, all of these have their goals, priorities and individual roles/tasks. If all these parts come together properly, the likelihood of success increases dramatically.

Time to Gel

As a leader, you may put 20 or 30 people together, give them each a role to play and call them a team. However, that doesn't mean that those 20 or 30 people will now function as a team. Remember, my expectation of my teams has been that (in addition to being productive, effective, efficient) when they go out among other folks and other organizations, they support one another, defend one another and are prepared to step up for the team and its members. That won't happen overnight. Be patient. Remember, that there are generally four stages of team development:

Forming—When the team first comes together, individuals tend to be cautious, try to be accepted and avoid conflict. They try to learn as much about the other members as possible and try to achieve something as a group. It doesn't happen automatically. It takes time. The leader's role is to guide them, to encourage them and to give them direction and purpose.

Storming—Confrontations gradually come to the surface and if the team is to grow, develop and be productive, these conflicts must be dealt with in a constructive fashion. It's time to aim for a win-win resolution not a win-lose one. The leader in this case must help the team work through the conflicts and become a solid unit.

Norming—Rules of engagement become clear and individuals get to know each other better. They should now be listening and completely understanding respective points of view. The group now begins to feel like a "team" and will resist any attempts to change it.

Performing—This is the stage where the group has identity, loyalty and high morale. There is a very comfortable level of operating and the energies of the group are focused on the task at hand. This is when the team is at its most productive state.

As a result, if you are the leader of a relatively new team, give the members time to gel, bond and get to know one another. Make sure they understand your expectations and be prepared to deal with anyone that turns out to be counterproductive to the overall team function or spirit. They don't need to be best friends and not every member will have a "rah-rah" type of personality. However, each may find, with your help, their own niche and make their own contribution. They will get to know each other better and understand each other's strengths and weaknesses. It's up to you, as the group leader, to help shape that bonding process.

Being a Team Leader

Every team in every possible situation needs leadership. To be successful, leaders need to perform a number of very important roles for the team. Those roles include, in no particular order, the following:

Decision Maker

For your team to be successful, it needs to have a mechanism for decision making and for everyone to know and understand the nature of that mechanism. The whole team must be aware of the extent of individual or sub-group empowerment. Conversely, if all decisions rest on your shoulders, as the leader, make sure all parties understand how the decision making process works.

Educator, Not a Blame Assigner

One of my favourite cartoons is a *Dilbert* (Scott Adams) comic where Dogbert explains to two of the staff with him, "I'd like to kick off the project by assigning blame for its eventual failure." What I truly love about this comic, besides Dilbert, is that even though it might be a bit exaggerated at times, the cartoons all too often reflect organizational realities. Leaders of good teams don't assign blame, at least not publicly. You can be certain that some things will go wrong. The leader and the entire team may need to know and understand why things went wrong, examine the causes and determine how to fix the situation. Going through this sort of exercise is part of a leader's role as an educator. Once you have learned from your mistakes and failures, move on and make sure it doesn't happen again.

Please note that I said not to assign blame publicly because if your group functions as a good team, all that really matters is that something went wrong and action was taken to resolve it. If the cause was a mistake made by an individual member, address it as a performance management or disciplinary issue, and do it behind closed doors.

Mediator

In the same way that "stuff" happens and things will go wrong, conflict is also bound to arise from time to time. Don't be surprised or alarmed. Also remember that a certain amount of conflict comes from different members having differing ideas, thoughts, suggestions and proposed solutions. This may actually be a good thing because it can lead to greater creativity in solving very complex problems. However, on occasion, if conflict escalates to the point that it threatens team chemistry, then it needs to be dealt with. In that regard, it is important to nip it in the bud early, prevent it from becoming hurtful or personal in nature and, to every extent possible, allow the members to self-identify the problems and, through open, honest dialogue, bring about a more effective solution. The leader may ultimately need to step in but should try to resist the temptation to solve all conflicts.

Communicator

I have already, at length, discussed the importance of effective communication. All the same principles apply in this instance. Meetings will be a fact of life for any team and that team's effectiveness will be enhanced by establishing solid communication habits for all members. Make sure everyone practices honest, respectful communications (this is especially true for the leader—you are a role model) and good, active listening skills. As a leader you will be occasionally faced with a group or team with its share of difficult personalities—the quiet one who doesn't say too much; the loud mouth who does say too much or tries to say it louder than everyone else (as if it's the loudest one who wins the game); the negative Nellie; plus a multitude of other disruptive personality types. Control them and encourage the team to monitor their own conduct and promote positive communication practices from each member.

Trainer and Developer of Staff

Remember that the focus and intent of this chapter is to promote the importance of supporting one another. Acting as a team is a critical part of that but there is more for a leader to do. Regardless of the sector or the nature of your role as a leader, you need to be a role model for others to follow, be it your staff, your colleagues, your students or your family. In that regard, never stop learning and developing yourself. If you are a manager, you have a responsibility to develop the skills, abilities and competencies of your staff. This starts with a simple performance management system. Forget, for the moment, everything you currently believe about performance management. It is one of the most unpopular organizational activities that one department (HR) can ever impose on other departments. Think of it instead as a means of communication with staff and developing their skills and potential for future growth. Forget the forms. They're not that important. (But don't tell your HR department that I said so.)

The key features of whatever system you use are that goals are set and reviewed through regular discussions and that development plans are created and monitored on a regular basis. A regular basis could suggest monthly, but that is not critical. Bi-monthly or quarterly may work just as well. The development plans may include courses, conferences, seminars or just reading assignments. They could include mentoring opportunities (having a junior employee work closely with and learn from a more senior member of staff), job shadowing, coaching or cross training. In each case, the intent is to develop the skills and interests of staff and to support them in their personal growth plans. However, beware of perceptions of favouritism for certain staff. They all deserve support and development. It's just that some may want the opportunities more than others. It is best not to favour those individuals over all others, and it is important to remember that not all staff want to grow in the business. Some may be both happy and productive in their current role. They can still be supported in their day-to-day activities.

For the parents who are now wondering if this has anything to do with you or even for those of you who are leaders in community organizations, the principles still apply. We need to talk with our kids regularly so they can understand us and we can understand them. Good communications means promoting the development of your kids. Your key role is to help them grow into outstanding adults. In fact, parents would do well to communicate more effectively with one another and help each other learn and grow. If you are the Rotary Club president, it behooves you to develop others to be able to step up into your shoes someday. The neighbourhood hockey coach has a responsibility to help his/her players grow, not only in the sport but as people too. All of us, as leaders, have a role to give back and one of the most meaningful ways we can do that is to help other members of our team meet their fullest potential.

Counsellor and Mentor

Members of your family or your team may need you to counsel them from time to time and help them with both personal and work-related issues. You don't need to be a professional counsellor but you do need to keep an open door (figuratively and literally) as well as a sympathetic ear and heart. On occasion, the leader will need to step up as a mentor for younger members or new members of the team. Accept this role with relish. It is important.

Facilitator

Occasionally, others may come to you for help in areas that you initially believe may have nothing to do with you. Always be prepared to do what you can to assist them anyway. It's part of being nice to others and may be seen as part of your role as leader. Over the years, I have had staff or others come to me for advice about exploring opportunities in other departments or even within other organizations. I could have said "It's your problem not mine" but I didn't do that. Instead, if I could help them gather information, arrange meetings or interviews or even act as a reference, I was happy to facilitate their growth and development as people. I may lose someone to another department or organization, but as a leader, I truly believe that I have at least helped them out.

It's Time to Celebrate!!

What does celebrating have to do with supporting one another? I speak and write often about the importance of reward and recognition programs. If used properly, these programs most assuredly demonstrate a commitment to staff and a way of supporting them in their efforts. But staff can also, if properly encouraged by the leaders, support each other by celebrating birthdays, recognizing outstanding personal or team efforts, posting congratulatory messages or letters as well as any other effort that serves to simply pat a colleague on the back as a gesture of appreciation and respect. These are not the only initiatives that work. There are doubtlessly hundreds of others, many of which are tailored to each organization's unique situation and characteristics. Don't hesitate to try anything once. Sometimes the effort alone is what is appreciated by your team and, remember, this doesn't have to be your initiative exclusively. Anything you can do to promote team members supporting and recognizing one another will pay you back tenfold, at home, in the community and at work.

Principle # 9

Scan the Horizon

In 1980, singer/songwriter, Harry Chapin, wrote a song called *Flowers Are Red*, a song that was intended to be critical of our educational system. However, it also implored us to open our minds to other possibilities and other visions of reality. As he noted, flowers are not always red but they come in all of the colors of the rainbow. If there is one constant in our world it is that there is always change going on. There is always something new and different with some wondrous possibilities. The things that are as we know them today may not be the same a year from now. While there are some who would long for "the good old days" (I am often one of them), the reality is that we need to first acknowledge that change will happen, then anticipate what that change may look like and, finally, take steps to adapt to the changes and enjoy the ride.

If you are a leader for your people, whoever they may be, you need to keep an eye on the horizon in order to see other possibilities or perhaps a new world that may exist beyond your immediate field of vision. The status quo is comfortable. It is what we are familiar with. However, regardless of our own comfort zone, the world is ever changing and we must be prepared to not only change with it but also to lead it. Martin Luther King Jr. had a dream that envisioned whites and blacks as equals in a fair and just world. John F. Kennedy had a dream of seeing a man on the moon by 1970. Bill Gates saw "a computer in every home." While, in each case, the world may not have witnessed a complete fulfillment of those dreams, we have certainly moved far along the road to their realization. Had the dreams not been there in the first place, there is a good possibility that racial segregation would still be the order of the day, much as it was in the 1950s. The space program would not have evolved to the same degree as it has and the world of computers would not be where it is today.

Leaders need to dream, to have a vision and to perpetually scan the horizon. We need to see every colour in the rainbow, not just the reds and greens. Failure to see alternatives or failure by leaders to have any vision of a different world in which they currently live will result not only in struggling along with the status quo but in their department, service, organization or even their family going backwards relative to everybody else. As it states in the Book of Proverbs, Chapter 29, Verse 18, "Where there is no vision, the people perish." Alternatively, in a more modern vein, consider the words of Larry Spears when contemplating the visionary nature of servant leadership:

> The characteristics of conceptualization and foresight are particularly important for servant leaders . . . They must balance the need to empower others with the need to be strong, visionary, transformational leaders. It demands that leaders be aware of their individual situations, that they listen to others, conceptualize the big picture, and persuade and empower others to lend their own talents in fulfilling the mission of the organization. In this way, servant leaders are not victims of their organizations and the people they lead; they are the co-creators of the future. They must seek to find ways to create win/win situations, which ensure that all concerned—leader, staff, organization, and customer—survive and thrive.[15]

Managers scan the horizon at work as part of their normal routines as they prepare budgets, business plans and resource needs for both the short and long term. Organizational leaders must keep an eye on future trends and changing industry norms. Community leaders need to look to and plan for the future in order to ensure that community services continue to be appropriate and sustainable. Family leaders need to be aware of future financial needs for their homes and their families. They also need to consider appropriate education plans for their children and to prepare for their retirement years. All of these activities involve scanning the horizon and much of that revolves around anticipating and planning for change.

Change Happens

As I have noted, change is the only constant in our lives. It happens to all of us, and when it does, we need to get on with it. Change may threaten things that we are comfortable with and that we have invested our time, energy and money into creating. It may be the introduction of new computer games, a new boss, a new job routine or even changes in community leadership or direction. I enjoy the small community that I currently live in but have recently become aware that a development of some 20,000 has been approved. This does not sit well with me but whining about it will not make the situation any better for me or my family. My grandchildren know more about computers than I will ever hope to know. This also does not sit well with my ego. However, once again, I can't think of these issues as problems and I have the power to turn these into challenges or opportunities. Perhaps, I should have seen them coming in the first place, which leads me to the point of needing to anticipate change.

Anticipate Change

I regularly encourage others to engage in "slow leadership" and take time to enjoy life and smell the roses. We should savour each and every day as it happens and not worry too much about next year or five years from now. However, that does not mean that we ignore the signs about what may be coming our way. As leaders, we need to seek out signs of new trends, opportunities and risks both in our professional lives and in our personal lives. Again, this doesn't mean that we focus exclusively on the future at the expense of enjoying the present. My advice is to take time around the beginning of the year to both reflect on what has been happening and to cast our minds forward to what we expect for the next year, but this can't be a once-a-year sort of activity. Read the papers and magazines (not the gossip rags but legitimate papers, journals and magazines), track the news reports, see what the stories on the internet are telling us, listen to the experts. Keep abreast of the political, environmental, economic and social trends and try to understand how they will affect you, your staff and your family. What are the signs telling us? Where are the opportunities for us at home and at work? What risks should we be aware of? When we have a sense for all of this, we need to plan accordingly, which simply means we need to adapt to the changes happening around us.

Adapting to Change

If you anticipate and monitor changes that are happening in your world, adapting to those changes will be less problematic. When the goalposts change, we need to change our game plan accordingly. Try to be proactive and be at the front line of the new order of things. Oh, how I wish I had been more excited about the possibilities in the new computer age. If I had, I would have been far more comfortable with technology than I currently am. However, hindsight is perfect so there is no sense bemoaning what I did or did not do in the past.

Enjoy the Ride

Things will never go back to the way they were so we need to regularly get out of our comfort zone and enjoy the new order of things. They will certainly be different but the role of the leader is to help others adapt to the new order. Attitude is so important. When change happens, look at the glass as being half full, not half empty. As somebody once noted, "Without change, there would be no butterflies." Enjoy each and every moment of each and every day. If you, as a leader, enjoy the changes that happen to you, there is a good possibility that all those around you will enjoy the ride a little bit more.

Leaders and Vision

Earlier, I discussed the differences between management and leadership. Management involves planning, organizing, implementing, controlling and delegating (or some such combination of functions) but a pure manager is less inclined to have visions and dreams. Managers who serve as effective leaders will perpetually scan the horizon and will have a vision about how much better their department, service or organization may be. In many ways, leaders will see the big picture and focus on so much more than just the financial and business elements. They consider spiritual and emotional aspects of making things better for themselves as well as for those who rely on them for their leadership skills, be that at home or at work. Remember that a key function of leaders is to inspire others to greater achievements or to increased personal heights. Their visions need to grab the attention and commitment of others. How does this happen?

So, Exactly Where Are You Headed?

Stephen R. Covey in *The 7 Habits of Highly Effective People* speaks of the need to begin with the end in mind. Generally, when we plan to take a trip, we know our starting point and we know our final destination. That is like beginning with the end in mind. Others speak of the practice of developing *big hairy audacious goals* (BHAG's). Either way, we, as leaders, need to stretch our boundaries and our horizons by considering possibilities beyond our current realities. Under the conditions as we now know them, what do we see in the future? Trying to determine what that future looks like is the leader's role and that requires some foresight, some good guesses and an understanding of the environment in which you work. We need to be able to assess and analyse trends and what those trends may mean for our business. We need to let our imagination run wild.

The municipality where I currently reside expects to double its population in the next 25 years. What will that mean in terms of services? How will that, in turn, affect municipal operations? What other work and life trends do I need to be aware of? How does the newest generation of workers approach work generally? Is it the same as the baby boomers? Notwithstanding the fact that there are currently high unemployment rates, the experts keep telling us that we will experience labour shortages in the not-too-distant future. How will that affect us? If the municipality doubles in size, will its workforce also double in size? What specialties will we need? How will technology affect the workplace and our homes?

Regardless of your work environment, be it human resources, automobile manufacturing, consulting, shoe sales, making widgets or looking after family matters, these are the types of questions that you need to be asking every day and even when you have answered them, they need to be asked again. You need to not just ask the questions but you also need to stay abreast of what the experts are saying and always get the input of your staff as well as any others that may be affected by the future trends and your response to those trends. Remember what I said about the importance of the team. You can't be a one person band! It's a perpetual cycle of activity and you must be prepared because, although you may think you know where the goal line is today, I can guarantee you that the goalposts are always being moved, especially when you think you are getting close.

Big Hairy Audacious Goals

Now that you've asked all the questions that must be asked, you need to set some goals. These are not the type of goals that a manager and an employee set during the annual performance appraisal. It's not a matter of tinkering a bit, making one part of the organization a bit bigger or better or improving some other aspect of service. It's really about leaders stretching the boundaries and reaching for the stars. The goals that we personally set for ourselves (even our families) or those we set for our departments and organizations must be realistic but they also must be credible and, in fact, attractive and inspiring for others, especially for those who we expect to follow us and believe in us. We cannot simply dictate that "this is what I have decided that our new vision will be." A leader may have that sort of vision but getting others on board with it requires a certain amount of persuasion, influence and credibility with those being led.

Let's go back to Bill Gates' goal of having a computer in every home. When he first stated it, would it have been considered a stretch? Of course. If you worked with Bill Gates, would it be a goal you could get excited about? Absolutely. Did his company get behind him? You bet! All parts of an organization must work together to make the goal a reality.

For example, within an organization, the service departments need to be aware of the larger organizational goals and will set their own goals to match. For example, for an HR department, goals that generate some enthusiasm and some stretch may include:

- To become the acknowledged industry experts in HR management practices
- To have 100 percent electronic staff records
- To see a merged HR function involving our organization and five other related organizations

There is nothing magical about these goals, but they are realistic, credible and the staff are likely to find them attractive.

One example of a BHAG for a service organization was the Rotary Club International's goal of eradicating polio around the world. At the time it was first stated, it was a huge stretch. However, to all intents and purposes, the Rotary club has come close to achieving that goal. At a personal level, families aim to be debt free by a certain age or perhaps have a house bought and paid for by a given date. They may want to comfortably retire to the cottage by age 60 or ensure that they have enough money set aside for the kids' education costs by the time the kids go away to college or university.

A word of caution about setting BHAG's for your department or your organization. Remember that I have stressed the need for them to be realistic and they need to get people excited. In setting these goals, beware of offending organizational traditions and cultures. Organizations grow and evolve over the years as a result of the hard work and dedication of many people who have invested a great deal of their time and energy into making things the way they are today. Part of that evolution includes the growth of traditions and cultures that serve as an organizational identity, something that staff, both past and present, easily associate with. If you set a BHAG that breaks too dramatically from the past, not only will the goal be unattractive but it may be considered to be quite unreachable. It is bound to fail. For example, if General Motors leaders suddenly announced a future where they envision making furniture instead of cars (I know it's silly but stay with me), they will enjoy no organizational support whatsoever. Why? Because too many people have invested too much of their time and energy working for an automobile manufacturer to now switch to furniture. However, a future that envisions making only hybrid vehicles would likely be more realistic, credible and attractive for the organization and all the people working there.

What Does Goal Accomplishment Feel, Taste and Look Like?

It's time to set our BHAG's but how will we know if or when we get there or if we're at least part way there? If we go back to the General Motors example and we assume that it sets a goal of total hybrid production, progress will be quite measurable as each product line that converts to hybrid status will be one more step along the path. It is worth noting, at this juncture, that I have absolutely no expertise whatsoever in automobile manufacturing, so my example may be quite meaningless but I believe it at least serves as a reasonable illustration for the purposes of this discussion. On a personal level, I may set a goal of having a book on a best sellers list within 10 years. It certainly is attractive and I will know when success, as measured by that goal, has been achieved. But there are indicators along the way that will help me at least taste a modicum of success.

If we set a goal for 10 or 20 years in the future, remember that we must constantly scan the horizon and we must keep asking questions, the answers to which will serve to help us amend our goals as necessary. Those futuristic visions may change with time, but we certainly need to keep the big picture in mind as we establish mid—and short-term goals. Again, looking at a personal goal of having a book on a best sellers list in 10 years' time, a mid-term goal may be a book that sells 5,000 copies and a short-term goal may be to simply get published (yahoo!! at least one goal has been reached). If I hit those goals, I will have achieved success, both measurable and identifiable. But as I achieve them, the horizon may change again. That's okay. It still serves to keep me focused on the horizon.

Have Your Vision But Don't Forget to Stick to Your Values and Purpose

I have made it clear to this point that I believe every department, every organization and every individual should have core values that guide their every action and decision. Regardless of any growth, any changes in direction or any new demands, our values must remain pure and consistent. Similarly, the purpose of an HR department (for example) "to deliver the best possible service, advice and counsel in all related human resources functions to our client groups" won't change from one year to the next. Examples of other corporate values and purposes that will remain constant include:

Merck

Values:

- Corporate social responsibility
- Unequivocal excellence in all aspects of the company
- Science based innovation
- Honest and integrity
- Profit, but profit from work that benefits humanity

Purpose: To preserve and improve human life.

Walt Disney

Values:

- No cynicism
- Nurturing and promulgation of "wholesome American values"
- Creativity, dreams and imagination
- Fanatical attention to consistency and detail
- Preservation and control of the Disney magic

Purpose: To make people happy.

Sony

Values:

- Elevation of the Japanese culture and national status
- Being a pioneer—not following others; doing the impossible
- Encouraging individual ability and creativity

Purpose: To experience the joy of advancing and employing technology for the benefit of the public.

These companies have not strayed from their essential values and purposes. However, their visions always consider them and push the organization to achieve a little more.

Some Final Thoughts on Visioning

As a leader, you need to perpetually scan the horizon and the good leaders do just that. However, don't ever think that it is an activity that you need to do alone. In the same way that teams utilize the skills and abilities of many to make our work results more effective, involving your staff and others in visioning exercises will lead to more credible visions, greater acceptance and, ultimately, a more effective implementation program. As we consider visions and the subsequent plans, we need to contemplate how they will influence our people systems, leadership, internal and external relationships, the infrastructure, processes and systems. We need to do more than say "Here is my dream; my vision." We need to remember that our vision affects many others, so the tricky part is to make those dreams a reality.

Strategic Planning

Here is your chance to make your vision a reality. I suspect we have all been a part of doing a SWOT analysis. Consultants love it. For those readers who have not had the pleasure, SWOT refers to an exercise of examining our organizational or departmental **s**trengths, **w**eaknesses, **o**pportunities and threats. Essentially, we consider our internal environment (strengths and weaknesses) as well as the environment within which we function (opportunities and threats). Reviewing this information gives us the parameters for developing a long-range plan or a strategic plan to guide the department or organization. Add to these activities some form of collective dreaming or blue sky thinking, wherein we are allowed to simply say "in an ideal world under ideal circumstances, where do we see ourselves in 5, 10 or 20 years?" The collective dreaming part means we rely on others as well as ourselves to do the dreaming and the visioning.

We can use senior staff members or preferably, all staff members as well as other significant stakeholders. They are all part of the team so they need to all be part of the dream. It makes it more sellable. Thoughts are shared, without criticism initially. Anything goes. As alternative possibilities are developed, they are eventually evaluated and, if successful, prioritized. If they are not successful, it means they were not considered to be practical or realistic or affordable and again, remember, our visions must be credible and attractive. The process continues with the allocation of potential resources. Obviously, as each part of the plan unfolds, resource needs are refined and activities to monitor, measure and correct deviations as necessary are developed.

I have already alluded to the need to keep our visions flexible and meaningful. Becoming too entrenched in our strategic plans and not regularly reviewing and updating them could have negative results:

- An organization becomes locked in to unreasonable and unbearable long-term resource allocations, that is, the business shrinks due to a recession, long-term leases based on what may have been unrealistic plans could become crippling.
- Forgetting to perform our roles with excellence on a day-to-day basis. We become so attracted to the long term that we miss out on the everyday. We no longer see the forest for the trees.
- Increased staff cynicism when dreams don't come to fruition. The attitude becomes "What a silly waste of time that was. What's next, I wonder?"

- The business becomes less adaptable in a rapidly changing business environment. Things change so quickly that leaders need to remain flexible and nimble allowing them to respond quickly and effectively to changing circumstances. Becoming too entrenched in a strategic plan may hinder this flexibility.

Don't let long-term dreams, visions and plans become an anchor for you. They should be there to guide you, not to drag you down.

Implementation of Plans

As I said in the last section, involving staff and others in the dreaming part of your vision is important. This involvement helps to generate ideas and possibilities and sell new concepts that will lead to achieving full implementation of the new plan or vision. In order to achieve the best possible value in a strategic plan or new direction, it is best to consider three factors.

First, a new plan or vision cannot be issued as an edict. The team is once again critical. Get your team's input as well as that of clients through focus groups or surveys and maintain their input by involving at least some members in steering committee activities. Put the question to them: "How can we most effectively roll out **our** plan to the organization?" Create sub-committees for different features of the plan. Assign leadership roles to different individuals. The search for input must be sincere and the leader must be credible.

Second, communicate, communicate, communicate. Let folks know what the strategic goals are, how you arrived at them, where you are headed and when. Identify some key messages to be delivered. Ensure that focus groups get feedback regarding their input. Celebrate successes and milestone events. Will a retreat for key stakeholders help? Sometimes, they can be extremely effective and, at other times, a waste of time. Consider the group and what may be achieved.

Third, no matter how positive or exciting your message and your new vision may be, expect some resistance. You may personally have doubts (or perhaps, just questions about how good an idea this really is) in much the same way as your staff and colleagues do, especially if your new vision takes you in a new direction or into relatively uncharted territory. This is new. Will it work? Have we made accurate assumptions about the industry, our business or the economy generally? Any change means that something familiar will be lost and many of your staff, colleagues and even your own supervisor will find the status quo to be more comfortable than any possible new directions. Also, there may be practical implementation problems or the new direction may face challenges that were unanticipated. Motivation of staff could be difficult but none of this needs to be overwhelming or unmanageable. Just be prepared for resistance from any number of sources for any number of reasons and they may even make apparent good sense.

In the final analysis, as a leader, you have a responsibility to lead your people day in and day out. However, part of that responsibility goes further, to consider the future, perpetually scanning the horizon and grabbing the attention and commitment of others as you move towards the achievement of that vision.

Principle #10

Have Fun, Be Nice, But Make Decisions

This is one of my favourite stories. Once upon a time, an old man, a young boy and a donkey set out on a long journey on a very hot, dry summer's day. They passed a group of travellers and, as they passed, heard comments about it being a shame that the old man was making the young boy walk on such a hot day and it would be far better if he were riding on the donkey. The man and the boy discussed the comments, agreed, put the boy on the donkey and continued on their way. Shortly after, they passed another group and heard comments about it being unfair that the boy was riding while the old man had to walk. Again, they discussed the comments and, again, agreed to change the arrangements. The old man joined the boy on the donkey and they proceeded. Soon enough, they passed another group of travellers and heard comments about how badly they were treating the donkey, making him carry them both on such a hot, dry day. Once again they discussed the comments and this time, one of them picked up the front end of the donkey and the other one picked up the other end and away they went. However, as they crossed a bridge over a raging river, they tripped and dropped the donkey into the river and it was never seen again. The moral to this story is if you try to please all of the people all of the time, you might as well kiss your ass goodbye.

Leadership involves making decisions. Leaders also face conflict on a regular basis and decisions must be made about how to deal with those conflicts.

In actual fact, decision making and dealing with conflicts are two sides of the same coin. In both cases, choices must be made. Alternatives must be considered. Differences of opinion must be faced and addressed.

What Is Involved in Decision Making?

Let's not kid ourselves. No matter how we slice it, the process of making decisions seldom follows a neat, step-by-step routine. Most of the decisions we make almost seem spontaneous in the face of all the decisions that need to be made on a daily basis. While the experts may not agree on the exact number and nature of steps in the decision-making process, there is some general agreement on what happens each time a decision is made.

For my purposes, let's keep it simple and I would like to suggest the following as an appropriate decision-making model to follow:

1. Determine the exact nature of the problem
2. Generate alternative solutions
3. Evaluate each alternative
4. Select and decide
5. Implement the Decision
6. Monitor and follow-up

Let's look at each of my six steps in order.

Determine the Exact Nature of the Problem

The best way to get to the root of the decision to be made is to consider the 5Ws—who, what, why, when, where. Again, this is not critical for many of our daily decisions. If somebody wants to paint your office and the decision to be made is "what colour?" going through the 5Ws is something like going after a fly with a shotgun. It's a bit of overkill. However, when a major player in the automobile industry, decides to change or to eliminate a complete line, the company no doubt faces a number of questions. Working through the 5Ws would help the leadership of the company reach their decision.

If you're struggling with a decision, ask the questions in order to reach a fuller understanding of the issue. Obviously, with more complex situations, more people may need to be involved. Don't hesitate to involve them as necessary. Many decisions affect many people and a leader will often face situations where different people are recommending different courses of action. Remember that your decision must reflect **what** is right, not **who** is right. You can't please everyone. Your role as a leader is to make the best decision for the organization, the company or your particular situation.

Generate Alternative Solutions

If we go back to the office painting situation, the only alternatives we face are to do nothing or to pick a colour. It's really quite simple. However, for GM, as one of the major players in the auto industry, when its very existence is at stake as well as billions of dollars and scores of affected stakeholders, I'm reasonably sure that the company's leadership doesn't decide to eliminate a line over a cup of coffee or the flip of a coin. Doing nothing could be catastrophic and may negatively impact the company's ongoing success or viability, yet that may legitimately be one of the alternatives being considered. In all likelihood, dozens of other alternatives will be considered before the leadership settles on the ones that work best for the company and its stakeholders.

In the HR world, if an organization is facing an increasing number of grievances, deciding on how to best deal with that situation will generate a number of possible alternatives. These will range from doing nothing to meeting with the unions, analyzing the core problems, providing training to managers and bolstering HR staffing. Once again, the decision may not involve a single action but a "package" of actions. More complex problems call for more complex decisions.

Evaluate Each Alternative

Evaluative criteria for any situation or organization may include any or all of the following:

- Budgetary impact—both capital and human costs
- Return on any investment
- Ethical considerations
- Whether it's legal
- Risk assessment—for investment, reputation, legal challenges, etc.
- Time required
- Feasibility of success
- Impact on customers or other stakeholders
- Impact on the community or competition
- Plus any other factor that may be peculiar to your own industry or situation

This type of evaluative process occurs on a daily basis covering everything from deciding when and where to go on the family vacation to hospitals considering what mix of services they need to provide in order to best address the demands of the community they serve. A service club needs to allocate limited resources to different projects and therefore, they need to evaluate all the options open to them. Union leadership can't propose all the changes their membership wants in the next collective agreement but they will evaluate all proposals and make a decision about what will go forward in bargaining. Part of the role of any leader is that you must evaluate options in order to make the best possible decision.

Select and Decide

You make your decision based on the entire analysis of the alternatives you have available and using all the information you have at your disposal. It sure is tough sometimes but that's why you get paid the big bucks, and for those of you acting in voluntary leadership capacities, that's why you are where you are. It's no different for parents. Parents are expected to make the decision. Sometimes you may not have every piece of information that you may like to have, but eventually you have to ask if you have enough information. I do not want to encourage hasty decision-making practices nor do I want to suggest waiting an inordinate length of time while more information arrives (more on these problems later), but the time must come to make a decision. Do it and hope for the best.

It's important to note that despite our best intentions—and despite the wealth of information that we contemplate before making our decision, the many stakeholders we involve, the alternatives we consider and the final decision-making steps we follow—we sometimes make bad or wrong decisions! I know it's hard to imagine but I've done it myself. So what is to be done? Well, stuff happens and we have to deal with it. It becomes another decision to make. Digging your heels in and standing by your original decision, just on a matter of principal, may not be the best idea. This is when you need to be a little more flexible.

This type of mistake happens on a regular basis when we make hiring or promotion decisions. Sometimes, they are a crapshoot at best. We may hire or promote somebody who, by all accounts and indicators, should be perfect. It doesn't work out that way. You can stand by the original decision for a period of time and try to make it work but sometimes, we arrive at a point of no return and we have to admit that a mistake was made. Cut your losses. Deal with it and try again. Better to admit you made a mistake and are taking steps to correct it than to live with the mistake in perpetuity.

Implement the Decision

Let all affected parties and stakeholders know what the decision is. Depending on its level of complexity, the communication of the decision can be straightforward or complicated. In the case of the office painting decision, you likely only need to let the painter know the decision. Nobody else is likely to really care. However, in more complex scenarios, the communication plan could involve staff, customers, unions, boards, shareholders and the general public. The rollout of the decision also requires a plan, which could include determining the roles to be played by those involved with the decision's implementation. Assign tasks, responsibilities, timelines and reporting relationships to accomplish the delivery successfully.

Monitor and Follow-up

This is part of your job. You've made a decision. Now, make sure it happens. Tasks and timelines have been assigned. Keep an eye on things to see that what is supposed to happen actually does happen. If something goes off the rails, take appropriate action to get it back on track. Treat these types of actions as more decisions to be made.

Decision-Making Challenges (or What Drives Your Staff and Colleagues Crazy)

There are few things that will drive your staff and followers crazier than poor decision-making habits. Most of us can live with or tolerate the occasional wrong decision, but some other habits are unforgivable. Ask yourself if you fall into any of the following traps.

1. Trying to Please Everyone

Most of us would probably appreciate spending our remaining years on this earth making everyone we come into contact with happy. Wouldn't that be great? Unfortunately, like the old man, the young boy and the donkey, it's not realistic and, usually, it just doesn't work well. Consensus works when a team arrives at a decision that every member wholly supports and every member is willing to do their part to implement. But that is often not the case and, occasionally, as a leader, you will be in a position to hear from all members, consider everyone's input and then, make the decision. The important role that you play in this scenario is ensuring that everyone's voice and opinion are properly heard and considered. You don't have to rehash issues ad nauseam in order to try to achieve consensus. Remember: You can't please all the people all of the time.

2. Procrastination

Usually, procrastination goes hand in glove with trying to please everyone, but it may often be a mechanism we use for the simple, day-to-day decisions we all face. When you need to make a decision, consult with everyone you need to hear from, consider the pros and cons and make a decision. Avoid putting it off. Procrastination can turn people off, significantly increase your workload and result in a huge waste of your precious time because it usually results in your handling issues more than once.

3. No Decision

If you fail to make a decision, you're not delaying or deferring or even procrastinating, you may be pretending that the decision having to be made doesn't exist. This approach is akin to sticking our head in the sand and hoping it will go away, and is particularly true in conflict situations in which many of us feel uncomfortable. However, not making a decision is, in essence, a decision not to act. That is contrary to your role as leader.

4. Being Too Hasty

While making expeditious decisions is something I like to promote, you need to be certain that you have enough information to make sound decisions. Constantly flying by the seat of your pants and making hasty or ill-informed decisions can only lead to mistakes and inevitably an increase in the workload for you and everyone else as you scramble to undo the damage done and start all over again. That's if you're lucky. There is no single, simple answer as to when you have enough information and when waiting for more is simply wasting time. You need to determine for yourself when you have enough information and can make a balanced decision.

5. Is It Your Decision to Make?

Regardless of whether we are making decisions that our staff should make or overstepping our own limitations, making a decision that should be made by someone else can be a big problem. It is a morale buster if we don't respect our staff or others and fail to empower them. They must be allowed to make many decisions on their own. Also, setting aside the morale issue, it may be just, plain and simple, inefficient. Barry Rand, former CEO of Avis, once said, "If you have a 'Yes man' working for you, one of you is redundant." If you are making decisions that others should be allowed to make, one of you isn't needed. Similarly, crossing the line to make decisions that your boss should be making or for which you don't have the expertise, could be a disaster waiting to happen. Worse yet, it could be very career limiting. Make sure the right people make the right decisions at the right time.

Group Issues and Effective Team Decisions

Many of the situations contemplated thus far have focused on the leader who is responsible for making many decisions on a daily basis. Some decisions are the leaders alone to make while others need the input, co-operation and implementation support of many others. While group decision situations are many and varied, it is most common to use them primarily for more complex or important matters. These would be cases where two or more heads are better than one. Often, we have access to a multiplicity of skills, abilities, knowledge and expertise that we may not otherwise have. In addition, following a group discussion/decision process can lead to greater acceptance of the decision, stronger group buy-in and ease of implementation. But beware, the dreaded committee may rear its ugly head and, while the reputation of committees has generally been sullied over the years (often with just cause), the use of a group process remains an effective tool in decision making.

The steps to making decisions via a group remain the same. We must still determine the problem, generate alternatives, evaluate those alternatives, decide, implement and monitor. The biggest challenge is to ensure that you have the right people available to make the best decision. For that purpose, you need critical thinkers with a variety of related skills who are not afraid to challenge (always respectfully) one another, and, in fact, be challenged by others. Patrick Lencioni, in *The Five Dysfunctions of a Team*, suggests, among other things, that effective teams demonstrate the following:

- They trust each other and take full, positive advantage of their collective strengths. Further, they give each other the benefit of any doubts, are willing to challenge, don't engage in politics and work as a group.
- Engage in meaningful conflict by keeping meetings interesting and lively and draw on ideas of all team members. They do not aim to harm one another.
- When a decision is made, they are all committed to the decision and its full implementation.
- Hold one another accountable to perform at all times at the highest possible standard without any excess of bureaucracy.

- All members are achievement and goal oriented. They expect to accomplish something and not just spin their wheels.[16]

Notwithstanding the tremendous value that may be derived from effective teams, it is wise to be cognizant of the following group challenges. First, we need to beware of what is called the Abilene Paradox, an expression first coined by Jerry Harvey in 1988. It describes a situation where a team agrees upon a particular decision but only because its members believe that is what the other members of the team want. The result is that they engage in a process that none of them may really believe in. They get frustrated, blame one another for the apparent miscommunications and achieve nothing productive. There is no accountability, no commitment, no success and most important, there has been no honest and open communication with one another.

Second, is the potential to experience "groupthink," a situation where individuals go along with a decision or line of reasoning because they want to be part of the group, want to agree with the leader or because they are disengaged. The result is, again, a lack of true commitment to the team.

Third, excessive individualism occurs when team members really don't give a damn about "the team" and are there only to advocate for their own individual interests. These people fail to see the big picture and meetings often deteriorate into arguments and general disarray.

If any of these situations exist for your team, they need to be dealt with or you will fall into a perpetual state of mediocrity at best, and, more likely, plain old inefficiency will be the order of the day and the committee will, once again, have earned its negative reputation.

Meeting Types

Lance Goosen's cartoon in this chapter is a rendering of the meeting types that all of us have seen (or worse, recognize as ourselves) and many of them, unfortunately, don't contribute much to the quality or success of our meetings. These types include all of the following and perhaps some others as well (in no particular order):

Wise Owl: This is the one you want in attendance. He is not particularly emotional but will engage in meaningful, helpful dialogue, doing his best to ensure that the meeting is productive. I know we all see ourselves in this role but . . .

The Quiet One: This one may be brilliant. We don't really know for sure because she doesn't say anything. She contributes nothing to the discussion, good or bad, and, as a result, seems to only occupy space that may be better used for something a tad more productive.

The Loud Mouth: If volume was a measure of quality in contributing to the team discussion, this one would be great. Too boisterous. Too loud. Too overbearing. Turns everyone off. Your ears hurt at the end of the meeting.

The Great Talker: May not necessarily be loud but talks too much and loves to tell the old war stories. "I remember back in George's day when we used to blah, blah, blah . . . ." He keeps the meeting going interminably by commenting ad nauseam about every topic and wanting, too often, to go down memory lane. Stick to the issues at hand!

The Know It All: If you have an idea, hers is better. You pick the topic and she knows everything there is to know about it and, at the very least, has a friend or colleague that does. Always plays the game of one-upmanship.

The Class Clown: We need a little comic relief from time to time but enough already. Yes, I'm the one who said it's important to have fun but we need to accomplish something, so let's get serious for at least a part of the meeting.

The Official (not really) Critic: He criticizes everything but offers nothing constructive in return. When an idea comes forward, he tries diligently to find something wrong with it as opposed to seeing the goodness in everything. His glass is perpetually half empty.

The Disengaged: Like the Quiet One, she contributes nothing to discussions. Unlike the Quiet One, who we weren't really sure about, we know this one doesn't want to be there and she is not in tune with the rest of the group.

The Advocate: Unfortunately, he doesn't advocate for the team but for his own personal agenda. He aggressively pursues his own position and issues, completely disregarding other opinions or the common good.

The Back Stabber: This one has similarities to the Official Critic in that she is usually critical of others but, in this case, she is sniping from cover. Just when you think she's on board with an idea is when she is most dangerous. She may take credit for the achievements or contributions of others or may just attack them without justification. Certainly, she is not a team player.

These people may not be found in every group but watch for them, especially in teams that do not function well. That's where you are most likely to find them.

Conflict and Decision Making

This is not a discussion on conflict management. I'll save that for another day. However, conflict is something every leader will face from time to time and, during those conflict situations (which are not necessarily always bad or negative), decisions must be made. This applies to every leader of any kind from the family to the hospital auxiliary to companies to organizations.

The Nature of Conflict

No matter what size of organization you may be a part of, one with a few staff to one with 20,000 staff or even within a family unit, it is almost inevitable that conflict will arise from time to time. The North American workforce is becoming increasingly diverse and includes all races, creeds, sexual orientations and ages. Within each workplace, there are differing opinions about values, goals, objectives and even mundane matters such as politics or yesterday's soccer game. There may be conflict over these issues and sometimes they are exacerbated by overlaps in job functions, scarce resources, power relationships, poor leadership, ambiguous roles, performance issues and poor communications. If conflict is allowed to exist unchecked, it has the potential to adversely affect productivity, absenteeism, customer relations and labour relations generally. As a result, huge dollars are spent annually simply trying to counteract the impact felt in the organization by unresolved conflict.

Causes of Conflict

As noted, some of the common sources of conflict include:

- Poor communications
- Ambiguous roles
- Limited resources
- Differing personal values or interests
- Performance concerns
- Personality clashes

Sadly, what contributes to conflict almost as much as anything is the failure of leadership to deal with it in the first place. Doing nothing simply exacerbates the problem and frustrates all participants as well as other staff, customers, volunteers, and others in the workplace.

What To Do About Conflict?

There are two things that need special consideration when one contemplates the matter of conflict. First, conflict, as noted, is not necessarily bad. A difference of opinion between two or more individuals may generate innovative solutions to common problems. It can lead to positive change, process improvements, greater efficiencies and stronger interpersonal relationships. The status quo will be challenged. Conversely, if allowed to fester, conflicts can have negative ramifications throughout the workplace.

It is important that a leader confronts the conflict immediately and directly. Avoiding it may seem like a good idea at the time (only because confrontation is so difficult for many of us) but the reality is that avoidance will eventually come back to bite us and usually at the most inopportune time. Actions that leaders can take in addressing conflict more effectively include:

- Being a model of the behaviours that are desired. Make sure others understand the values you believe in and expect your behaviour and theirs to align with those values.
- Addressing underlying tensions. Promote open and honest communications. If there are issues that need to be addressed, talk about them.
- Providing more role clarity, especially where job roles and responsibilities may be the source of the conflict.
- Managing toxic individuals and dealing with them effectively. A toxic environment is not healthy for any of us and, in the workplace at least, those individuals responsible for the toxic environment because they are bullies or they have a poor attitude or values that are inconsistent with everybody else must be dealt with. They need to get on board or they must leave the organization.

Once again, decisions need to be made; avoidance is not an option.

So, what is it that a leader can do? The options available, in terms of relative cost, can range from prevention to arbitration or litigation, which are much more costly. In between those extremes are options for the use of internal or external mediation. While parties are often very certain they are "right" in a conflict and equally certain that an arbitrator or judge will clearly vindicate them, the reality is that there are no guarantees and going to court or to arbitration is time consuming, expensive and will almost invariably result in hurt feelings and damaged relations. It is never the preferred alternative if it can be at all avoided. However, on occasion, it is the last resort. Just don't be in a rush to get there.

Obviously, the best and most cost effective means of addressing conflict is to follow the old adage "An ounce of prevention is worth a pound of cure."

In that regard, policy development and education are key organizational initiatives that can most effectively address conflict by actually dealing with it before it happens.

We need to consider any conflict situation in light of the decision-making model noted previously. In particular, when we face a problematic conflict, we need to:

- Ensure a complete understanding of what the conflict is all about
- Generate alternative solutions
- Evaluate the solutions
- Select a course of action to address the conflict
- Implement the chosen course of action
- Monitor and follow-up as appropriate

The most important aspect of conflict management is that we manage conflict and make decisions to resolve it. Under no circumstance does it involve avoiding conflict. While avoidance may seem to be an easier course of action, it is never more productive, and it is not the course of action taken by a good leader.

Principle #11

Exude Energy and Enthusiasm

"Nothing is so contagious as enthusiasm."

—Samuel Taylor Coleridge

"Enthusiasm is the yeast that makes your hopes shine to the stars. Enthusiasm is the sparkle in your eyes, the swing in your gait, the grip of your hand, the irresistible surge of will and energy to execute your ideas."

—Henry Ford

Throughout this book, I have shared my rules for day-to-day leadership, everything from having fun to making decisions. However, it is questionable if any of them will make any difference whatsoever if you don't exude energy and enthusiasm. Consider, for a moment, some attributes of great leaders with whom you have worked, read about or even seen in the movies. What do you notice about their life habits or their work habits? In almost every instance, they work tirelessly for "the cause," regardless of whether their cause pays them or is something that is more driven by their heart and their spirit. It doesn't automatically hold that working long hours makes one a great leader. There are many people that I have personally known who have worked many hours of overtime every day and every week but I would not consider them to be great leaders by virtue of this fact. In some cases, they were simply inefficient. In other cases, they failed to delegate effectively or have been micromanagers. Some were under resourced for the job at hand, others overworked or just challenged in any number of other ways. I am not suggesting, by any stretch, that a leader must work huge amounts of overtime, with the obvious exception of parents who so often get no breaks at all.

But, let's consider the case of Nelson Mandela. For the most part, he was successful in leading the fight against apartheid in South Africa. Did he achieve it by working 9 to 5, five days a week? NO! Was Jack Welch able to turn around General Electric through a normal work week? Not likely. How about JFK? Mother Theresa? Erin Brokovitch? All of these individuals put their lives behind their cause.

Think about leaders you know. The theme is always the same. They have a cause that they feel is worth aiming for, that they believe strongly in and for which they work tirelessly. But it is more than just working long hours. They exude energy and enthusiasm. They exemplify a "can-do" attitude and apply it daily to achieving their purpose. They think positively about their goals and what is important about what they do. That positive thinking always takes them and their followers closer to the ultimate fulfillment of their collective dreams.

High energy and enthusiasm is not limited to high-profile people. If any of us drift through life, at home or at work, without exuding energy or enthusiasm for much of anything, you may rest assured that we will fail to inspire anybody. If, as I have stated, we are all considered to be leaders in some element of our lives, then we need to demonstrate an enthusiasm for something that is bigger than ourselves, something that we believe in strongly and are prepared to work tirelessly to achieve. For some, that happens at work. For others, it may be a community cause and for others still, it is all about making their life and that of their family something more memorable than mere existence.

If you are a leader, you need to have intensity of purpose and energy. If you don't you really won't be anything more than just another manager or just another passenger on a bus trip through life. Without a purpose, there is a possibility that you will not have what Kevin Cashman called "authentic followers." A certain amount of energy and enthusiasm is, of course, inherent in the personality of some people. They just seem to be more perpetually energized even if that energy is caused by a little too much coffee in the morning. However, everyone has the same potential to achieve a degree of that enthusiasm and some of that comes from what I describe as having fun. Recall that I spoke of the need to find something you really enjoy doing, something you really believe in and are prepared to pursue it tirelessly. We need to ask ourselves the following types of question:

1. What am I passionate about? For each of us there is something in life that is especially important. Perhaps we have been touched by cancer or some other disease and we want to help others in their battle. It may be that we see a need to clean up our community or improve the lives of the homeless. What is it for you?
2. Why do I pursue the worklife I do? Did you choose the career you did because it was meaningful for you, because it is something you really enjoy doing or did it just happen to you? Do you work at what you do just for a paycheque?
3. What are my gifts? Each individual has unique gifts that they bring to the world of work or at home or in the community. What are yours and how can you better share them with the world?
4. What energizes me most and, when I'm fully engaged in that activity, how does it make me feel?

The most effective leaders are those who are engaged in a line of work or a cause that they are passionate about. They are the ones who use their natural gifts in the achievement of their goals and who are particularly energized and enthusiastic about what they are doing. "Leaders are the most results-oriented individuals in the world, and results get attention. Their vision or intentions are compelling and pull people toward them. Intensity coupled with commitment is magnetic."[17] Isn't this what it's really all about? Encouraging others to share your vision and your passion and to really get behind you? That is what your energy and enthusiasm will truly accomplish.

Once again, let's forget about high-profile leaders and consider day-to-day examples of people we all know who fail to realize their full potential because of a lack of energy or others who achieve more than expected because they make up for their lack of God-given talent by a significantly increased dose of energy and enthusiasm. Many of us have children, friends, neighbours or staff we know who are blessed with high IQ's but whose lives have taken a wrong turn and they end up wasting their potential. They are often perceived to be lazy or shiftless by many and are eventually written off. "They could have been so great" becomes a familiar refrain. On the other hand, we all know of someone about whom we may say "not the sharpest knife in the drawer" but they make up for it in energy and enthusiasm. They often become good leaders with people happily following them.

Another characteristic that separates the good leaders from the also-rans and one that is routinely evident is that the good leaders always allow themselves to be guided by a power of positive thinking. Their glass, as previously noted, is always half full. But what does that really mean and how can we all learn to benefit from doing some more positive thinking? How important is attitude to the quality of our leadership?

Earlier, I commented on the gentlemen I worked with who were honest, hardworking and productive. If you recall, I said that once a week we would go out for lunch and talk about life and the world at large. The problem was that, invariably, the other two would sink into a trap of discussing all that was wrong with the world so much so that I ended up feeling down after the lunch. I would return to work and feel quite unproductive for the afternoon. What a waste. So, the moral to this story is to think positive thoughts, maintain a "can-do" attitude and you, as well as everyone with you, will feel and function better.

You see, there is an analogy used quite regularly by writers such as Hal Urban, Robin S. Sharma and others of the human mind as something of a fertile garden. If we plant good seeds (ideas and knowledge), maintain fertile soil (keep an open mind), feed the garden with study and learning and weed it regularly by removing any negative thoughts, we will enjoy a bountiful harvest. James Allen is an inspirational speaker and has this to say about the garden we keep:

> Just as the gardener cultivates his plot, keeping it free from weeds, and growing the flowers and fruits which he requires, so may a man tend the garden of his mind, weeding out all the wrong, useless and impure thoughts, and cultivating toward perfection the flowers and fruits of right, useful and pure thoughts. By pursuing this process, a man sooner or later discovers that he is the master-gardener of his soul, the director of his life.[18]

What is it that ordinary leaders can do to engage in the power of positive thinking?

First, consider how many times we see corporate leaders announce bad news, for example, extensive layoffs or plant closures, and then, as part of their announcement, portray the news as something that will "make us stronger in the long run." Or the tax increase that we are told we'll soon have to pay with the added qualification that it will make the community stronger and better positioned for the future. Maybe it's the new major capital investment or joint venture that "won't cost taxpayers a cent"!! My intent is not to judge whether or not the statements are true but to note that positive thinking can be a powerful leadership tool. We can always find the silver lining in any cloud. Find it and don't focus on the bad news. As I said previously, stuff happens. Deal with it. The people you lead want and need to hear the facts but they also want and need to be told that some good will come from bad news. Take every opportunity that you can to serve as a platform for good news. However, bear in mind that delivering the good news with the bad relies upon how authentic the audience believes their leader to be. If your reputation is one of being inauthentic, all the nice words in the world won't make a particle of difference. Being authentic in the first place will make these types of messages more powerful than ever.

Second, keep your mind open for any and all positive possibilities. Being told that you are facing a serious budget crunch in the upcoming fiscal year may be the opportunity you need to restructure your department in a way that is more beneficial to you, your staff and your customers. If a long-time member of your department decides to retire, look at it as an opportunity for positive change even though it will be a loss to your team. Even on the home front, losing a job may be devastating. On the other hand, it may be the opportunity you need to pursue a career choice that seems more exciting or take a new direction that you have always dreamed of. There is always hope.

Third, believe in yourself, always feeling empowered and in charge. You need to look in the mirror each and every morning and declare "Damn, I'm good and I'm gonna have a great day" (proper English is not necessary, especially first thing in the morning). Self-confidence and self-esteem do wonders for the power of positive thinking and will carry over to all those who work with and live with you. Frankly, a "woe is me" sort of attitude does not cut it nor is it allowed for leaders. You and you alone are responsible for your attitude. You must believe that you will succeed. You may be supported by others but, ultimately, it comes from you. From somewhere deep inside, you must always believe in your own ability to survive and thrive. Think of what can be, not what can't be. Don't be a victim of the Wallenda factor. Karl Wallenda was a tightrope aerialist who fell to his death in 1978. His wife later recalled that all Karl had worried about for months was falling. The seed was planted in his mind that he needed to be concerned about falling rather than succeeding. The same thing happens every time I golf. If I worry about putting the ball into the bunker, you can be certain that's where it will go. If I ignore the bunker, I enjoy a greater likelihood of success (although, not always).

Fourth, be persistent in the pursuit of things that are important without being unduly dogmatic. Good things will often not happen easily and there will always be naysayers and obstacles in your path. They may need to be convinced or they may need to be moved. Like a good boy scout (or girl guide) be prepared. Pursue things that are important to you with a spirit of adventure, enthusiasm and optimism.

Fifth, connect with other positive thinking people. I've already addressed the importance of relationships for a leader and now, I will qualify that by saying that you need to build relationships with the right people. Connect only with those that will prove to be of benefit for you, your family or your workplace. You don't need to cultivate any other relationships.

Sixth, as much as possible, keep the negative crap of the world out of your mind. I know it's nigh impossible sometimes, but try anyway. For many of us, when we first get up in the morning, the first thing we read is the daily paper or we watch the news on television or we go to the internet for an update on what's happening in the world. Typically, what sells newspapers is BAD NEWS. How many times do you hear people in the organization you are with remark about how fast and effectively bad news travels? How many times during each day do you let your mind wander to all the problems that you or others need to deal with? All this negativism is neither healthy nor productive. Try this sometime. Ignore the bad news. Stop reading the paper first thing. Try to turn it around, with every opportunity, to good news instead or, at least, the more positive aspects of the bad news, like the budget crunch that presents you with new opportunities. Fill your mind and your spirit with more positives.

Finally, you have visions, dreams and goals. Now, go out and act on them. Nobody will come along and simply say that your goals have been approved and everything you have wished for is hereby granted. If that happens to you, I want to know the name of your genie. You have to make them happen for yourself and that requires a dose of energy and enthusiasm. Take it and run with it.

Being a Leader

Up to this point, I have been stressing the importance of a leader's energy, enthusiasm and positive attitude. When I have met with or interviewed dynamic organizational leaders over the years, these factors have been accepted as being of critical importance to their success. While my own principles suggest that exuding energy and enthusiasm is of something all leaders should personify, there are other personal characteristics and traits that can combine quite effectively with this to make an even better leader. These traits, in whole or in part, have to be apparent to those people you are leading in order for you to be truly effective. Above all else, what has been mentioned almost universally has been the need for the right "attitude."

In addition, leaders need to be upbeat, positive, encouraging, inspiring, have guts, show courage, demonstrate calmness under fire, be open to new ideas and initiatives and be the ones who ultimately shape the organizational culture. When I was writing this book, I interviewed many organizational leaders, and these were the descriptions they used when answering my question "What is your role as a leader?" From their answers, several themes became evident and I would like to introduce them to you here:

- Leadership comes from a passion within. I'm not sure how to describe this any better. There must be a certain "fire" that you, as a leader, feel and demonstrate to others. You believe in what you do and it shows in everything you say and every action you take. It becomes so evident that your staff and others also feel it and are willing to become engaged in your cause.

- Consistency. A leader's mood and spirit don't rise and fall with the seasons or the days of the week. Every day is the same. Those issues that are important today are important tomorrow. The energy, mood and spirit never vary.

- Walk the talk. Lead by example. I can't promote a "do as I say; not as I do" type of philosophy. If I expect staff to be ethical, they must expect no less of me. If I want staff to be customer focused, I must be the same. If I want my kids to be respectful and courteous to others, they must learn by my example. There cannot be a double standard.

- Common sense. Unfortunately, common sense is far too uncommon but it is something we all need to exercise more often. Use and apply good, practical, common sense skills and use them consistently.

- Inspirational. This deserves special attention because it was mentioned so often and when one considers ways in which a leader can be inspirational, it was noted, that he/she always needs "to find the spark in each person." Remember to treat everyone else as an individual. We are all unique in this world. To find that unique spark in each of us is the challenge and it becomes a key skill for all leaders.

- Humble. A leader will make mistakes but he/she also admits when the mistakes are made. They are not pretentious and, above all, they are always respectful.

- Candor. You can always count on a good leader to be honest and up front with everyone they interact with. There are no false fronts or pretenses and no airs or deceits about them. They are authentic.

So, now that we know the sort of characteristics that are found in everyday leaders and now that we know the importance of exuding energy and enthusiasm at all times, what can we do to stimulate and maintain that energy, enthusiasm and positivism for ourselves and others?

Robin S. Sharma in *Leadership Wisdom from the Monk Who Sold His Ferrari*, addresses this very issue when he discusses what he calls the 5 Disciplines of Self Leadership.[19] These are the actions we can all take to keep ourselves mentally, spiritually and physically fit. These disciplines include what he refers to as personal renewal, abundant knowledge, physicality, early awakening and a deathbed mentality. Reflecting on each of these, I would add the following comments.

1. Personal Renewal: It is critical that we approach our role as leader with energy and enthusiasm. However, we cannot maintain that energy level in perpetuity without regular down times. We need to rest. Life and leadership are nothing more than a long journey during which we need regular pit stops. Nobody can be effective 100 percent of the time if they don't take daily breaks (enjoy the work/life balance I referred to earlier), getting a good night of sleep each and every day and **not** working, on a regular basis, seven days a week. Vacation time is of critical importance to us. Too many surveys and far too much is being written suggesting that too many of us are not taking our full vacation entitlement. When our leaders do not take their full entitlement, they wear it like some kind of a badge of honour. It is not healthy. It is not efficient and, frankly, it demonstrates a low standard in the quality of their leadership. If someone has to work year round without proper vacation, it is only a sign that something is wrong with their organization or their leadership skills.

2. Abundant Knowledge: The metaphor of the human mind as a fertile garden includes the need for good seeds, which are the ideas and knowledge that we have the capacity to receive into it each and every day. Sharma's book promotes the importance of reading (especially classic works) for 30 minutes each day. For my part, I don't care what you read but gather new ideas via whatever means you may choose, be it reading classics, newspapers, professional journals or even the internet. All have immense value and if you keep your mind as an open receptacle for new learning, your ability as a leader can only be enhanced. Never quit learning.

3. Physicality: Keep your body in shape. Like the First Discipline of Personal Renewal, the importance of exercise and maintaining a generally good level of fitness can never be overstated. At the very least, enjoy a brisk 30-minute walk every day. Go for a run if you still can. Play with your children or grandchildren. Stay active in sports. Personally, I walk and work out daily, play golf in the summer and hockey in the winter. Try tai chi, yoga, swimming, skiing or whatever else may tickle your fancy. Also, as part of the whole notion of staying in shape, come the eating routines that we engage in. Watch what you put in your mouth. Many of us (including yours truly) still eat too much and the wrong types of food. Far be it from me to promote absolute purity in our eating habits because I still enjoy a bowl of ice cream with my grandchildren from time to time. However, I still encourage you to watch carefully what you eat and drink and make sure that you exercise regularly. It's the only way to maintain appropriate health and good levels of energy.

4. Early Awakening: How much sleep do we really need and why do so many of us waste the first couple of hours of every day? Sleep is necessary for personal renewal but don't overdo it. Personally, I can't recall the last time I needed an alarm clock to wake up. Maybe it's a blessing and sometimes, when I want a little extra sleep, it's a bit of a curse. However, early morning is very peaceful and productive for me. Sometimes, I use the time to get a ton of quality work done (as I write this chapter for instance, it has just turned 7:00 AM) or, on most days, I use the time to go for a walk

and to work out. Get up, get going and enjoy the best time of day. Maybe there is something to that old saying "early to bed; early to rise".

5. Deathbed Mentality: Life is short. Enjoy each and every day that you have on this earth. As Emerson noted:

> To laugh often and love much; to win the respect of intelligent persons and the affection of children; to earn the approbation of honest critics; to appreciate beauty; to give of one's self, to leave the world a bit better; whether by a healthy child, a garden patch or a redeemed social condition; to have played and laughed with enthusiasm and sung with exultation; to know even one life has breathed easier because you have lived—that is to have succeeded.

For my part, I have often, when attending funerals, reflected upon what I would like a eulogy to say about me. I listen closely to what is being said about the deceased and know that, when my time comes, I hope that those in attendance will celebrate the life I shared with them and will be able to acknowledge that, to paraphrase Emerson, I have left the world a bit better place than when I first arrived in it.

Be healthy, be happy and approach everything you do with a spirit of optimism, adventure and enthusiasm. It is a childlike quality that so many of us, leaders included, have left behind. Think of our children and our grandchildren and how so many things, especially in their first few years, are so wondrous to them. We become adults. We become leaders. And, all too often, we forget how to revel in each and every day, in each new experience. Don't forget how to live life.

I keep three words written on my whiteboard in my office: Attitude, Gratitude and Action. I see those words every day and try diligently to follow them in my work life and my home life. They are words that guide me as a husband, father, manager, at home, at work and in the community. It is our collective attitude that determines whether or not we have fun at work, or for that matter, at home. So many of us fall into the trap of bemoaning how hard we have to work, how little we are appreciated, how we don't have enough of anything—money, power, supplies, equipment, staff and so on. However, it is our attitude that makes our work and our lives valuable, valued, memorable and a source of pride. I try to keep my attitude positive and follow my own principles including the ones about having fun and being nice. I am thankful for my life as well as those things and people that are an important part of my life such as my family, my health and so many things that we take for granted in Canada, the United States and other developed countries in the world. Remember that so many others, in undeveloped countries or regions, ravaged by war or disease, have much less to be thankful for.

Finally, I try not to just talk about doing this and accomplishing that in my lifetime. I make sure I act. I am prepared to make decisions and make things happen in my roles as a person and as a leader. Attitude. Gratitude. Action.

Concluding Remarks

Leadership is all about inspiration and each of us have the ability to inspire somebody else. For many, that happens at work. For others, it takes place at home. For those of us who have children, nothing could be more meaningful than to serve as a perpetual inspiration for our kids to the end of our days on this earth. The workplace and home are not the only places where we find examples of leadership. Some of us serve as leaders in the not for profit world, at church, in our unions, helping kids, serving seniors and a myriad of other possibilities. It is important to remember that leadership is not a one-time event. It is not like getting a certificate or degree whereupon someone considered to be all-wise or all-knowing confers his or her blessing on you and says "you are now a leader". We work at it, day in and day out. Alas, there is no magic formula to follow. It requires hard work, dedication, consistency and the application of a judicious amount of common sense. Following the principles found in this book will help measurably in this regard. There are those who will be inclined to tell me that "common sense isn't all that common any more". My answer to them is "In that case, let's work together to return to common sense". It can only happen one person, one action and one day at a time. As Mother Teresa once said, "Yesterday is gone. Tomorrow has not yet come. We have only today. Let us begin."

Endnotes

1   Peter M. Senge, "The Fifth Discipline" (New York: Doubleday, 2006), 328.

2   Jim Collins, "Good to Great" (New York, HarperCollins Publishers Inc., 2001), 20.

3   See Charles R. Swindoll at http://www.insight.org/

4   Kevin Freiberg and Jackie Freiberg, *NUTS! Southwest Airlines' Crazy Recipe for Business and Personal Success* (New York: Crown, 1998), 213.

5   Kevin Cashman, "Leadership From The Inside Out" (San Fransisco: Berrett-Koehler Publishers, 2008), 83.

6   David Weiss and Vince Molinaro, *The Leadership Gap: Building Leadership Capacity for Competitive Advantage* (New York: Wiley, 2005), 206-207.

7   Kent Nerburn, *Make Me an Instrument of Your Peace: Living in the Spirit of the Prayer of St. Francis* (New York: HarperOne, 1999). The story is posted at: http://www.huffingtonpost.com/kent-nerburn/cab-ride_b_1474147.html

8   Carter McNamara, *The Complete Guide to Ethics Management: An Ethics Toolkit for Managers* (CITY: Authenticity Consulting, 1997-2007), 5.

9   Michael Josephson, *The Six Pillars of Character,* as an article written in "The Ethics Edge; Second Edition" (Washington, ICMA Press, 2002), 11-17.

10   Stephen R. Covey, *The 7 Habits of Highly Effective People* (Philadelphia: Running Press Miniature Editions, 2000).

11   Tom Peters and Robert Waterman, *In Search of Excellence: Lessons from America's Best-Run Companies* (New York: Harpercollins, 2004).

12   Weiss and Molinaro, *The Leadership Gap, 58-61*

13   Freiberg and Freiberg, *NUTS!*, 149.

14   Peter S. Pande, "The Six Sigma Leader" (New York: McGraw-Hill Ryerson, 2007), 186.

15   Larry Spears and Michele Lawrence, eds., *Practicing Servant Leadership: Succeeding through Trust, Bravery and Forgiveness* (Indianapolis: The Greenleaf Center for Servant-Leadership, 2004), 151.

16   Patrick Lencioni, *The Five Dysfunctions of a Team: A Leadership Fable* (San Francisco: Jossey-Bass, 2002), 189-190.

17   Warren Bennis and Burt Nanus, "Leaders—Strategies For Taking Charge" (New York: Collins Business Essentials, 2007), 26.

18   James Allen, "As a Man Thinketh," http://jamesallen.wwwhubs.com/think.htm

19   Robin S. Sharma, *Leadership Wisdom from the Monk Who Sold His Ferrari: A Spiritual Fable About Fulfilling Your Dreams and Reaching Your Destiny* (New York: HarperCollins, 1998).